Highcharts Essentials

Create interactive data visualization charts with the
Highcharts JavaScript library

Bilal Shahid

BIRMINGHAM - MUMBAI

Highcharts Essentials

First published: October 2014

Production reference: 1241014

Published by Packt Publishing Ltd.
Livery Place
35 Livery Street
Birmingham B3 2PB, UK.

ISBN 978-1-78398-396-4

www.packtpub.com

Cover image by Faiz fattohi (faizfattohi@gmail.com)

Credits

Author
Bilal Shahid

Reviewers
Robert Blomdalen

Kurn J. La Montagne

Jugal Thakkar

Commissioning Editor
Ashwin Nair

Acquisition Editor
Neha Nagwekar

Content Development Editor
Sumeet Sawant

Technical Editors
Pratik More

Humera Shaikh

Copy Editors
Roshni Banerjee

Gladson Monteiro

Merilyn Pereira

Project Coordinator
Danuta Jones

Proofreaders
Simran Bhogal

Stephen Copestake

Ameesha Green

Paul Hindle

Indexers
Mariammal Chettiyar

Priya Sane

Production Coordinators
Arvindkumar Gupta

Komal Ramchandani

Alwin Roy

Cover Work
Komal Ramchandani

About the Author

Bilal Shahid is a web developer from Karachi, Pakistan. He has several years of experience with HTML, CSS, JavaScript, and PHP, and he also knows how to program in C and C++. He is passionate about the open source movement, and his interests include data-driven UIs, the real-time Web, and code optimization.

He was introduced to Highcharts while working on a big project dedicated to social media page management and analytics, and since then he has used it in several web projects.

He works for Traffic Group Ltd., the largest independent digital services provider in the Middle East, where he works as a senior UI developer. He likes to read books in his spare time.

About the Reviewers

Robert Blomdalen is a web developer who has worked with online systems since 2006. He is passionate about open source projects and has created a Highcharts library in PHP. Check out his profile on GitHub at `https://github.com/blomman9`.

Kurn J. La Montagne is a software engineer (with a strong preference for the Web), open source hacker, freelance developer, CakePHP Baker, and nature lover living in the tropical Caribbean island of Saint Lucia. He is employed as a web application developer with the National Insurance Corporation, where he enjoys working on a variety of web-based projects.

Prior to working with the National Insurance Corporation, Kurn studied Computer Science at the University of Southern Caribbean, Trinidad and Tobago, and was part of the team that won the first annual Teleios Code-Jam programming competition, an initiative of Teleios Systems Limited that encourages students to use information technology to solve problems and facilitate development in the Caribbean region.

He spends most of his free time hacking open source projects and is the creator of the CakePHP Highcharts plugin (available on GitHub). He enjoys working with many established frameworks as well as trying out new ones. He is currently working with CakePHP, Lithium, Yii, Laravel, and WordPress for various small projects. He is looking forward to branching out into Android mobile development, and his goal is to create the ultimate SaaS that will enhance people's lives. For the past 3 years, he has been lecturing part-time at the Saint Lucia extension campus of the University of the Southern Caribbean. He has also served as a technical reviewer for *Instant Fancybox*, *Packt Publishing*, and he is currently reviewing another video series on Highcharts that will be published soon.

I'd like to thank my wonderful family for putting up with all the busy hours and my incessant talking about things they don't really understand. My heartfelt thanks goes out to all the people who have assisted me grow as a developer and everyone who has offered guidance and encouragement, especially when the path ahead seemed blurry. I'd also like to thank the fantastic people at Packt Publishing for giving me the opportunity to contribute to this book.

Jugal Thakkar is a C# professional, JavaScript expert, and an Android fanboy. He forges user-friendly enterprise web applications and enjoys data crunching and visualization. He is passionate about mobile and web technologies and appreciates open source.

He has been an advocate of Highcharts since he got acquainted with it at work and now attempts to help developers on Stack Overflow. He occasionally blogs about Highcharts and has reviewed the recently published book, *Highcharts Cookbook*, *Packt Publishing*.

Jugal relishes playing ping-pong, solving puzzles, or trying his luck at a bowling alley. To know about what he learns, experiments with, and explores, visit `http://jugal.me/` or follow his blog, *A Humble Opinion*, at `http://ahumbleopinion.com/` (all the views expressed are his own and do not reflect those of his employer or anyone else).

www.PacktPub.com

Support files, eBooks, discount offers, and more

You might want to visit www.PacktPub.com for support files and downloads related to your book.

Did you know that Packt offers eBook versions of every book published, with PDF and ePub files available? You can upgrade to the eBook version at www.PacktPub.com and as a print book customer, you are entitled to a discount on the eBook copy. Get in touch with us at service@packtpub.com for more details.

At www.PacktPub.com, you can also read a collection of free technical articles, sign up for a range of free newsletters and receive exclusive discounts and offers on Packt books and eBooks.

http://PacktLib.PacktPub.com

Do you need instant solutions to your IT questions? PacktLib is Packt's online digital book library. Here, you can access, read and search across Packt's entire library of books.

Why subscribe?

- Fully searchable across every book published by Packt
- Copy and paste, print and bookmark content
- On demand and accessible via web browser

Free access for Packt account holders

If you have an account with Packt at www.PacktPub.com, you can use this to access PacktLib today and view nine entirely free books. Simply use your login credentials for immediate access.

Table of Contents

Preface	**1**
Chapter 1: Getting Started with Highcharts	**7**
Why choose Highcharts?	**7**
Plenty of chart types	7
Responsive	8
Dynamic	8
Deep browser support	8
Data preprocessing	8
Custom theming support	8
Multilingual	8
Extensibility	9
Installing Highcharts	**9**
A simple Highcharts example	**12**
Summary	**14**
Chapter 2: Column and Bar Charts	**15**
Introducing column charts	**15**
Using the official documentation of Highcharts	18
Including multiple data series	**18**
Stacking column charts	**20**
Column charts with normal stacking	20
Column charts with percentage stacking	22
Excluding a series from stacking	**24**
Drilling down the chart	**25**
Adjusting ticks and other chart elements	**29**
Introducing bar charts	**30**
Negatively stacked bar charts	**34**

Creating 3D column charts	**35**
Modifying the viewing frame	38
Summary	**39**
Chapter 3: Line and Spline Charts	**41**
Introducing line charts	**41**
Creating line charts with regular time intervals	**42**
Formatting date/time and data labels	44
Formatting the tooltip	46
Creating line charts with irregular time intervals	**48**
Creating line charts with multiple series	**50**
Loading data from an HTML table	**52**
Creating spline charts	**54**
Creating spline charts with plot bands	56
Combining line and column charts	**57**
Summary	**59**
Chapter 4: Area, Scatter, and Bubble Charts	**61**
Introducing area charts	**61**
Adjusting the placement of tick marks	63
Creating area charts with multiple series	63
Series with missing values	65
Sharing a tooltip between multiple series	66
Stacking charts with multiple series	**67**
Polishing the area chart	69
Area charts with percentage values	**72**
Area-spline charts	**73**
Introducing scatter charts	**74**
Formatting a tooltip with pointFormat	75
Scatter charts with multiple series	**76**
Creating bubble charts	**78**
Summary	**80**
Chapter 5: Pie, Polar, and Spider Web Charts	**81**
Introducing pie charts	**81**
Slicing off a pie chart	**84**
Enabling slicing by point selection	85
Drilling down the pie chart	**86**
Modifying the back button	88
Creating a 3D pie chart	89
Creating pie charts with multiple series	**90**

Creating a donut chart 92
Configuring a semicircle donut 95
Combining pie charts with line and column charts 97
Introducing a polar chart 100
Polar charts with different series types 103
Converting other chart types to the polar chart 104
Introducing the spider web chart 105
Creating a wind rose chart 107
Summary 110

Chapter 6: Other Chart Types 111
Creating an angular gauge chart 111
An angular gauge with dual axes 113
Styling the angular gauge 114
Creating a VU meter 117
Creating a solid gauge 119
Plotting a waterfall chart 121
Plotting a pyramid chart 124
Drawing a funnel chart 125
Creating a heat map 127
Fine-tuning the appearance 130
Formatting the tooltip 131
Summary 132

Chapter 7: Theming with Highcharts 133
Basic theming concepts 134
Formatting the tooltip with HTML 137
Altering borders, shadows, and backgrounds 140
Gradient fill types 141
Linear gradients 141
Gradient background for columns and tooltips 143
Linear gradients with multiple color stops 145
Radial gradients 146
Applying radial gradient to pie chart 147
Using Google Fonts with Highcharts 148
Using jQuery UI easing for series animation 150
Creating a global theme for our charts 151
Configuring our charts for internationalization 156
Summary 158

Chapter 8: Exploring Highcharts APIs and Events	**159**
An overview of Highcharts APIs and class model	**160**
Disabling the chart animation	163
Getting values with the Chart.get() method	**164**
Adding series and points	**165**
Adding a point dynamically	166
Adding a series dynamically	169
Adding drilldowns to series	171
Drilling up to the parent series	175
Accomplishing various tasks programmatically	**175**
Setting extreme values on an axis	175
Setting the chart title programmatically	176
Reflowing a chart	177
Destroying a chart	179
Hiding and showing a series programmatically	180
Highcharts events	**181**
Extending Highcharts	**181**
Adding custom event handlers	182
Wrapping prototype functions	183
Summary	**183**
Chapter 9: Going Further with Highcharts	**185**
Preprocessing data from different file types	**185**
Preprocessing data from a CSV file	186
Preprocessing data from an XML file	189
Preprocessing data from a JSON file	191
Preprocessing data from a database using PHP's PDO class	**192**
Fetching data and plotting the chart	193
Updating charts using Ajax	**197**
Exporting Highcharts into other formats	**202**
Exporting charts programmatically	203
Summary	**205**
Index	**207**

Preface

Highcharts is a JavaScript library for creating beautiful, interactive charts for the Web. It supports more than 20 chart types with various configuration options to help visualize data in a more robust way.

This book aims to be a fast-paced, step-by-step guide for anyone who is starting out with Highcharts. It presents information in a simple manner to help you get started with Highcharts in no time. References to the official documentation have been provided for you whenever a new concept is introduced to encourage you to dig deeper into the details.

You will be first exposed to simple concepts such as initializing different chart types and using their configuration options to modify their appearance and behavior. Once you have a solid foundation, we will move on to relatively advanced concepts, including Highcharts events and APIs. Finally, you will be presented with some additional techniques that involve working with stored and dynamically generated data.

By the end of this book, you will have a solid understanding of Highcharts and will be able to use it in different scenarios.

What this book covers

Chapter 1, *Getting Started with Highcharts*, describes Highcharts and its features. It covers basic installation of Highcharts with a working chart example.

Chapter 2, *Column and Bar Charts*, covers column and bar charts. It introduces the basic chart configuration options and shows how to configure a drilldown series.

Chapter 3, *Line and Spline Charts*, covers line and spline charts. It explains how different chart types can be combined to present data in a more understandable way.

Chapter 4, *Area, Scatter, and Bubble Charts*, describes the working of area, scatter, and bubble charts. It also introduces a new Highcharts feature: creating 3D charts.

Chapter 5, *Pie, Polar, and Spider Web Charts*, gives a step-by-step guide on working with basic pie charts and then configuring them to create a drilldown series. After that, polar and spider web charts will be explained.

Chapter 6, *Other Chart Types*, covers different chart types that are not covered in the previous chapters, including gauges, waterfall chart, pyramid chart, funnel chart, and heat maps.

Chapter 7, *Theming with Highcharts*, covers different aspects of modifying the appearance of Highcharts. It shows how to create a global chart theme, how to use Google web fonts, and how to use jQuery UI easing for chart loading effects.

Chapter 8, *Exploring Highcharts APIs and Events*, explains the usage of the robust yet simple APIs that Highcharts provides. At the end of this chapter, you will be provided with a foundation to work with Highcharts events and extend Highcharts.

Chapter 9, *Going Further with Highcharts*, includes different techniques to work with data from various sources and export Highcharts into various formats.

What you need for this book

You should have a working knowledge of HTML, CSS, and JavaScript. It is also preferred — but not required — to have knowledge of a server-side programming language, as we will be manipulating databases later in this book.

The following are the requirements:

- You must have PHP on your computer. This can be done by installing WAMP (http://wampserver.com), XAMPP (https://www.apachefriends.org), or LAMP (https://bitnami.com/stack/lamp/installer).
- You must have a modern web browser such as Chrome, Firefox, IE, or Opera.

Who this book is for

This book is for developers who are just starting out with Highcharts JavaScript library to create interactive charts for their web applications. It also serves as a guide for developers who have knowledge of other JavaScript charting libraries and are willing to migrate to Highcharts.

Conventions

In this book, you will find a number of styles of text that distinguish between different kinds of information. Here are some examples of these styles, and an explanation of their meaning.

Code words in text, database table names, folder names, filenames, file extensions, pathnames, dummy URLs, user input, and Twitter handles are shown as follows: "The Date.UTC() method used in the series component is the native JavaScript method that takes in date/time and returns the Unix timestamp."

A block of code is set as follows:

```
(function() {

  $( '#chart_container' ).highcharts({
    chart: {
      type: 'line'
    },
    title: {
      text: 'Vehicles Manufactured in the UK'
    },
    subtitle: {
      text: 'Source: <a href="http://www.oica.net/">OICA</a>',
      useHTML: true
    },
    data: {
      table: document.getElementById( 'vehicle_data' )
    }
  });

})();
```

New terms and **important words** are shown in bold. Words that you see on the screen, in menus or dialog boxes for example, appear in the text like this: "When the **Shortcut** window is closed, click on **Save** to save the changes."

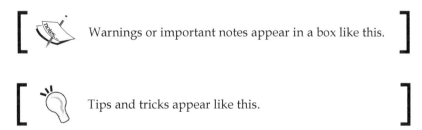

Warnings or important notes appear in a box like this.

Tips and tricks appear like this.

Reader feedback

Feedback from our readers is always welcome. Let us know what you think about this book—what you liked or may have disliked. Reader feedback is important for us to develop titles that you really get the most out of.

To send us general feedback, simply send an e-mail to feedback@packtpub.com, and mention the book title via the subject of your message.

If there is a topic that you have expertise in and you are interested in either writing or contributing to a book, see our author guide on www.packtpub.com/authors.

Customer support

Now that you are the proud owner of a Packt book, we have a number of things to help you to get the most from your purchase.

Downloading the example code

You can download the example code files for all Packt books you have purchased from your account at http://www.packtpub.com. If you purchased this book elsewhere, you can visit http://www.packtpub.com/support and register to have the files e-mailed directly to you.

Downloading the color images of this book

We also provide you with a PDF file that has color images of the screenshots/diagrams used in this book. The color images will help you better understand the changes in the output. You can download this file from: https://www.packtpub.com/sites/default/files/downloads/3964OS_Graphics.pdf.

Errata

Although we have taken every care to ensure the accuracy of our content, mistakes do happen. If you find a mistake in one of our books—maybe a mistake in the text or the code—we would be grateful if you would report this to us. By doing so, you can save other readers from frustration and help us improve subsequent versions of this book. If you find any errata, please report them by visiting `http://www.packtpub.com/submit-errata`, selecting your book, clicking on the **errata submission form** link, and entering the details of your errata. Once your errata are verified, your submission will be accepted and the errata will be uploaded on our website, or added to any list of existing errata, under the Errata section of that title. Any existing errata can be viewed by selecting your title from `http://www.packtpub.com/support`.

Piracy

Piracy of copyright material on the Internet is an ongoing problem across all media. At Packt, we take the protection of our copyright and licenses very seriously. If you come across any illegal copies of our works, in any form, on the Internet, please provide us with the location address or website name immediately so that we can pursue a remedy.

Please contact us at `copyright@packtpub.com` with a link to the suspected pirated material.

We appreciate your help in protecting our authors, and our ability to bring you valuable content.

Questions

You can contact us at `questions@packtpub.com` if you are having a problem with any aspect of the book, and we will do our best to address it.

1
Getting Started with Highcharts

Highcharts is a JavaScript library that adds interactive charts to websites or web applications. It supports more than 20 chart types that can further be combined into different combinations to make data more meaningful. Highcharts comes with a plethora of features, and yet its API is simple enough to get beginners up and running.

In this chapter, we will present an overview of Highcharts and its various features. We will take a look at the advantages that Highcharts offers over its alternatives and how it can help us with visualizing data by providing deep browser support and extensibility. We will also learn how to install Highcharts and familiarize ourselves with the file structure and different modules. At the end of this chapter, we will construct a simple column chart to kick-start our coding journey and get hands-on experience with Highcharts configurations.

Why choose Highcharts?

While there are other charting libraries available in the market, and some of them come with really nice features, Highcharts has its own place in JavaScript charting. Here are some of the Highcharts features that make it stand out from its competitors.

Plenty of chart types

Highcharts supports more than 20 chart types, and these include common chart types such as column chart, bar chart, pie chart, and area chart as well as advanced chart types including angular gauges, scatter charts, and range charts. If that's not enough for plotting the data, Highcharts also supports combining these chart types into various combinations for a more meaningful representation of data.

Responsive

Highcharts looks great in any screen resolution or size. Be it a desktop or a handheld device, Highcharts adjusts itself according to the viewport.

Dynamic

Highcharts supports dynamic plotting of data. Series can be added or removed and axes can be modified at any time after the creation of the chart. Charts can be updated constantly with data streaming from the server or being supplied by the user.

Deep browser support

Highcharts works on all modern browsers including Chrome, Mozilla, Internet Explorer, Netscape, and Safari. Legacy versions of Internet Explorer including IE6 and 7 are also supported by Highcharts.

Highcharts takes full advantage of the **Scalable Vector Graphics** (**SVG**) feature in modern browsers in order to render charts. In older browsers, it makes use of **Vector Markup Language** (**VML**) to draw the graphics. For Android 2.x devices, it uses Canvas to render graphics. When talking about performance, SVG gives the best results followed by VML and then Canvas.

Data preprocessing

When working with a large amount of data, it is not viable to write it in the form of static code. So, the data in CSV, XML, or JSON can be preprocessed before it can be plotted by Highcharts. Highcharts can also take preprocessed data from a database.

Custom theming support

While Highcharts comes with eight predefined themes that can be easily modified, it can be completely rebranded. Custom themes can be created by merely defining a JavaScript object with colors and fonts passed as values to their respective elements.

Multilingual

Highcharts allows charts to be presented in any language. Since it uses SVG for plotting the charts, support for bidirectional text is built right into it.

Extensibility

Highcharts comes with a great many features to make charting much more intuitive and elegant, yet it provides a simple API model to extend the core to include more features and support according to one's needs.

Installing Highcharts

In order to use Highcharts, we first need to download it. Go to `http://www.highcharts.com/download` and click on the **Highcharts 4.x.x** download button at the center of the screen.

It will take you to the download page. There are two options for the download:

- Download the full Highcharts package in `.zip` format
- Build the custom package to be downloaded by the Highcharts download builder

Downloading the full package will get you all the chart types, modules, adapters, themes, and other extra features. The full package also includes examples for using Highcharts and setting up the export server with different platforms to export charts to various image formats. The full package is great for learning and development purposes as it combines all Highcharts' features in one place.

If you need to use only specific features of Highcharts, then it's recommended to include only those specific files in your production code. This is where the download builder comes in handy as it presents various options as to what to include in the final download package. For instance, if you only intend to use the line chart type, then you can check that option and leave the others blank. Similarly, if you don't wish to use the drilldown feature, you can leave it blank to keep the code clean and minimal; hence, only the features meant to be used will be selected and only that code will be compiled into a single file, which can then be included in the production code. The download builder also includes an option to minify the code. If you wish to know more about Highcharts' features, you can refer to the actual documentation on the official site at `http://www.highcharts.com/docs`.

DOWNLOAD BUILDER (EXPERIMENTAL)

BUILD ☑ Compile code

Please note that at the time of writing this book, the Highcharts download builder is still in an experimental state.

For the sake of learning, download the full Highcharts package from the first option.

Extract the `Highcharts-4.x.x.zip` file somewhere on your hard drive. You will see multiple directories inside the top-level directory.

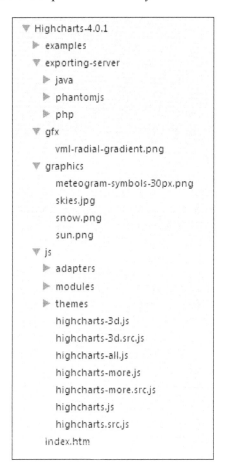

Each directory and its contents are defined as follows:

- `index.html`: This is the main demo file where you get to view various Highcharts demos. The demos of all chart types currently supported by Highcharts are listed on this page in the form of links preceded by the heading that specifies the chart type. You can quickly familiarize yourself with various chart types and how they look in the browser.

- `examples`: This is the directory where all the example files reside further in their respective directories. You can view the code of each example by going into the respective folder and opening the `.html` file in your code editor. Feel free to modify the code to see how it impacts the demo chart.

- `exporting-server`: This directory contains examples for setting up your own server to export Highcharts to various image formats. Currently, Highcharts supports export to `.png`, `.jpeg`, `.pdf`, and `.svg` formats. The examples included in this directory contain code to set up the exporting server in PHP, Java, or PhantomJS environments.

- `gfx` and `graphics`: These directories contain image files used by Highcharts examples.

- `js`: This is the main directory where all the Highcharts code resides. Here you will find JavaScript files with `.src.js` and `.js` extensions. The `.src.js` files contain the full code with comments, while the `.js` files contain a minified version of the code. You might want to use `.js` files in your production environment. Besides these JavaScript files, this directory contains three more directories:

    - `adapters`: This directory contains files to use Highcharts with frameworks other than jQuery, such as Prototype or MooTools.

    - `modules`: This directory contains several modules to add more features to Highcharts. These include the canvas module to support SVG on Android 2.x, the data module to make working with CSV or table data easier, drilldown to drill down the chart, and the exporting module for client-side exporting and printing of charts. Other modules included are the funnel, heatmap, solid gauge, and no-data modules.

    - `themes`: These are predefined themes with different settings of colors, fonts, borders, and shadows. Currently, eight themes are included in this directory, which you can use to quickly style your charts.

In order to use Highcharts, we need to include the jQuery library and the `Highcharts-4.x.x/js/Highcharts.js` file in our HTML code.

At the time of writing this book, Highcharts supports adapters for libraries that include jQuery, MooTools, and Prototype. In addition to these libraries, Highcharts also offers a standalone version for Vanilla JavaScript that can be downloaded via the download builder. The standalone adapter is the slimmest of all and is intended to be used with sites with limited bandwidth or in cases where the code is required to be as minimal as possible. Since every other site uses jQuery these days, we will use the jQuery adapter for our examples in the rest of this book. After having taken a good look at the important directories and files the package includes, let's get our hands dirty with the first working example of Highcharts.

A simple Highcharts example

In this example, we will create a basic column chart to show the GDP of the European Union from the year 2009 through 2013.

Let's start by creating a blank HTML file and then including jQuery and `highcharts.js` in the footer:

```
<!doctype html>
<html lang="en">
<head>
  <meta charset="UTF-8">
  <title>Highcharts Essentials</title>
</head>
<body>

<script src="http://ajax.googleapis.com/ajax/libs/jquery/1.11.1/
jquery.min.js"></script>
<script src="js/highcharts.js"></script>
</body>
</html>
```

Downloading the example code

You can download the example code files for all Packt books you have purchased from your account at http://www.packtpub.com. If you purchased this book elsewhere, you can visit http://www. packtpub.com/support and register to have the files e-mailed directly to you.

We have included Version 1.11.1 of jQuery from the Google CDN.

In the next step, we will create a container for our chart with `id` set to `highcharts_01`:

```
<div id="highchart_01" style="width: 600px; height: 450px;"></div>
```

We also gave the container element some basic CSS styles.

Having included the required JavaScript files and created the container element, we can now initialize Highcharts in a self-executing anonymous function, as shown in the following code:

```
(function() {

  $( '#highchart_01' ).highcharts({
    title: {
```

```
      text: 'GDP of European Union'
    },
    chart: {
      type: 'column'
    },
    xAxis: {
      title: {
        text: 'Years'
      },
      categories: ['2009', '2010', '2011', '2012', '2013']
    },
    yAxis: {
      title: {
        text: 'GDP'
      }
    },
    series: [
      {
        name: 'GDP',
        data: [-4.5, 2.0, 1.6, -0.4, 0.1]
      }
    ]
  });
})();
```

Refresh the page and you will be presented with a clean column chart, as shown in the following screenshot:

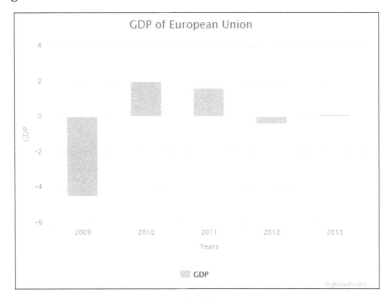

We first referenced our container element with jQuery, `$('#highcharts_01')`, and invoked the Highcharts function passed with a configuration object. The hierarchy of this configuration object is pretty simple. Each component of the configuration object corresponds to the structure of the chart.

We first set the title by setting the `text` property of `title` to `GDP of European Union`, and it appeared at the top of the chart. Then, we specified the type of chart we are rendering by passing `column` as the value to the `type` property of the chart.

The next two properties correspond to the axes of the chart, that is, the x axis and y axis. We specified the title of both axes the same way we did for the chart title. The years from 2009 through 2013 were specified as an array of `categories` on the x axis. These years appear at the bottom of the chart below the x axis.

Finally, the data to be plotted was passed to the `series` component. This data was passed in the form of an array with each element corresponding to the `categories` element as passed for the x axis.

Summary

In this very first chapter, we took a look at Highcharts and the features it provides to make JavaScript charting more intuitive and interactive. We also took a brief look at the options available when downloading Highcharts. After downloading the full Highcharts package, we familiarized ourselves with the included files and their purpose. At the end, we built a simple Highcharts to get started with this wonderful charting library.

In the next chapter, we will look more closely at column and bar charts. We will learn about configuring column/bar charts to enable the drilldown features that allow us to zoom in to the data. We will also learn how to stack column charts and create charts with negative stacks.

2

Column and Bar Charts

In the previous chapter, we discussed Highcharts and its features. We also took a look at the files that come with the package and then constructed a simple column chart to get started with Highcharts development.

In this chapter, we will examine column and bar charts more thoroughly and utilize the Highcharts API to make a variety of charts with different configuration options. To be more specific, in this chapter, we will:

- Take an overview of column charts
- Stack basic column charts to make data visually more understandable
- Learn how to configure charts to drill down to more detailed charts
- Adjust ticks and other chart elements
- Create bar charts
- Configure bar charts with negative stacks

Introducing column charts

Column charts are the most common type of charts. They have categories organized horizontally on the x axis (for example, time) and data is placed vertically on the y axis. They are useful for illustrating the difference between the data of each category.

Consider the London Olympics 2012 medal table, in which the top five countries are as follows:

Rank	Country	Gold	Silver	Bronze	Total
1	United States	46	29	29	104
2	China	38	27	23	88
3	Great Britain	29	17	19	65
4	Russian Federation	24	26	32	82
5	South Korea	13	8	7	28

The preceding list shows the gold, silver, and bronze medals won by the top five countries. The last column shows the total number of medals won by the respective country. We will plot this data into a column chart for a more meaningful visualization:

1. Create a new blank HTML file that includes the jQuery and `highcharts.js` scripts. You can also copy the HTML code from the example in the previous chapter. Note that the chart container element has the value of the `id` attribute of `medal_table`:

```
<div id="medal_table" style="width: 600px;
  height: 450px;"></div>
```

2. Place the following code in your `<script></script>` tags or the external JavaScript file if you are using one:

```
(function() {
  $( '#medal_table' ).highcharts({
    chart: {
      type: 'column'
    },
    title: {
      text: 'Olympics 2012 Medal Table'
    },
    subtitle: {
      text: 'Source: http://www.bbc.com/sport/olympics/2012/
medals/countries'
    },
    xAxis: {
      title: {
        text: 'Countries'
      },
      categories: ['United States', 'China', 'Russian Federation',
'Great Britain', 'South Korea']
    },
```

```
    yAxis: {
      title: {
        text: 'Number of total medals'
      }
    },
    series: [{
      name: 'Medals',
      data: [104, 88, 82, 65, 28]
    }]
  });
})();
```

The preceding code will produce the following column chart:

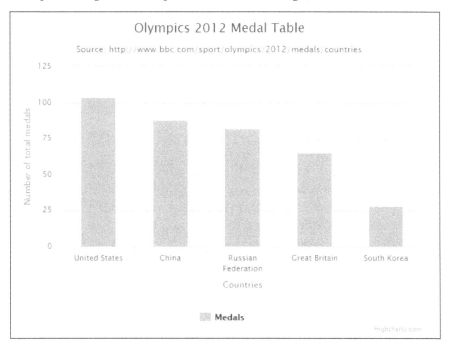

The preceding chart shows the total number of medals earned by each country. By referring to the total medal count, we include the numbers of gold, silver, and bronze medals.

In the previous example, we gave a subtitle to the chart using the subtitle property that points towards the source of the plotted data. The subtitle will appear below the main chart title. Also, note that both the *x* axis and *y* axis have their respective titles given to them via the title property. By hovering over each column, you can see the tooltip showing the category name (in this case, the country) and the value representing the data point.

The tooltip for the Great Britain series is as follows:

The preceding example shows the simplicity of the Highcharts configuration structure, which follows a hierarchical pattern. Each top-level component receives its own set of configuration objects comprising of its properties and their respective values. We will look at these additional properties in just a moment, but let's first modify the preceding chart to show multiple series.

Using the official documentation of Highcharts

By the end of this example, you might be willing to learn more about Highcharts components and their properties. For that purpose, the Highcharts website includes a robust documentation section that provides information about all the functionalities that Highcharts offers. This includes Highcharts components and their properties, methods, and events. You can find the Highcharts documentation at http://api.highcharts.com/highcharts.

The documentation presents information about Highcharts components and their properties in a hierarchical manner, thus making it a lot easier to find a specific property or method for a component.

Detailed documentation is accompanied by code examples in JS Fiddle that you can modify on the fly and see the results instantly.

Including multiple data series

Since the previous chart only shows the total number of medals, it's not very helpful when looking for the numbers of gold, silver, or bronze medals earned by each country. We can modify the chart to show the individual numbers while retaining its simplicity.

Copy the code from the previous example and modify the code to include an array of multiple series:

```
series: [{
  name: 'Gold',
  data: [46, 38, 24, 29, 13]
}, {
  name: 'Silver',
  data: [29, 27, 26, 17, 8]
}, {
  name: 'Bronze',
  data: [29, 23, 32, 19, 7]
}]
```

This modification of code will result in a chart showing the number of gold, silver, and bronze medals for each country.

As mentioned earlier, you can always navigate to the Highcharts documentation to find more about the series component at `http://api.highcharts.com/highcharts#series`.

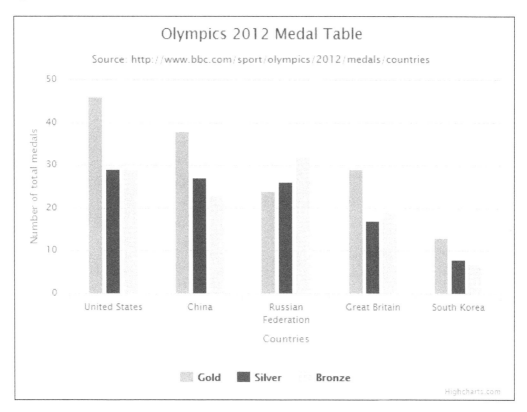

You can toggle the display of each series by clicking on the legend corresponding to each category at the bottom of the chart.

In this example, we included multiple series in a single chart to show a more simplified form of data. In the next example, we will stack these multiple series in a single column to show the difference in ratios between each category as well as visualize their total values.

Stacking column charts

There are two types of stacking in Highcharts:

- Normal stacking
- Percentage stacking

Let's have a look at the normal stacking of column charts in the following sections.

Column charts with normal stacking

Normal stacking stacks the data series on top of each other. This is a great way to visualize the total value of each category while showing any underlying data.

Copy the code of the first example of this chapter and modify the JavaScript to include the `plotOptions` component, as shown in the following code:

```
(function() {
  $( '#medal_table' ).highcharts({
    chart: {
      type: 'column'
    },
    title: {
      text: 'Olympics 2012 Medal Table'
    },
    subtitle: {
      text: 'Source: http://www.bbc.com/sport/olympics/2012/medals/
countries'
    },
    xAxis: {
```

```
      title: {
        text: 'Countries'
      },
      categories: ['United States', 'China', 'Russian Federation',
        'Great Britain', 'South Korea']
    },
    yAxis: {
      title: {
        text: 'Number of total medals'
      }
    },
    series: [{
      name: 'Gold',
      data: [46, 38, 24, 29, 13]
    }, {
      name: 'Silver',
      data: [29, 27, 26, 17, 8]
    }, {
      name: 'Bronze',
      data: [29, 23, 32, 19, 7]
    }],
    plotOptions: {
      column: {
        stacking: 'normal'
      }
    }
  });
})();
```

We configured the chart to stack data series by passing `normal` to the `stacking` property, and hence we were introduced to a new Highcharts configuration object, that is, `plotOptions`.

> The `plotOptions` component contains options related to the plotting of charts, including chart animations, chart display, and other user interaction properties. You can find more about it by visiting `http://api.highcharts.com/highcharts#plotOptions`.

The resulting chart will look like the following:

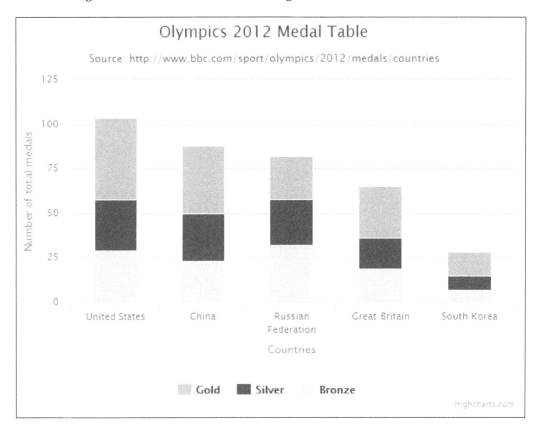

By looking at the chart, one can get a quick overview of the total number of medals each country won and in turn can also determine the count for the type of medals for each country.

You can also exclude a particular series from the stacking context if you wish to show it in a different column.

Column charts with percentage stacking

Configuring a column chart for percentage stacking is useful to visualize the ratio of each data series for a given category. It's just a matter of passing `percent` to the `stacking` property to make a column chart stack with percentages.

Copy the code from the previous example and remove the `stacking: null` property from the **Bronze** series to include it back in the stacking context. Change the `plotOptions` component to the following:

```
plotOptions: {
  column: {
    stacking: 'percent'
  }
}
```

The chart will now show stacked columns based on their proportions:

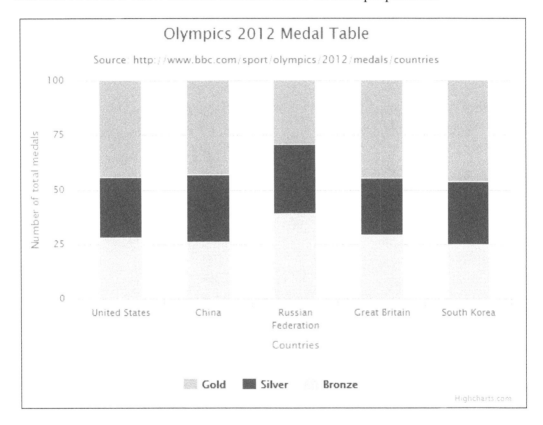

Percentage stacking calculates the proportion of each data point in the series relative to the sum of all data points.

While stacking is a great feature, it should not be used for a large amount of data series or it will make the chart look overly saturated, making the data visualization difficult. To get more details when working with large and variable numbers of data series, you should use the drilldown feature.

Excluding a series from stacking

We can also exclude a particular series from stacking by passing `null` to its `stacking` property, as shown in the following code:

```
series: [{
  name: 'Gold',
  data: [46, 38, 24, 29, 13]
}, {
  name: 'Silver',
  data: [29, 27, 26, 17, 8]
}, {
  name: 'Bronze',
  data: [29, 23, 32, 19, 7],
  stacking: null
}]
```

The **Bronze** series will now be excluded from the stacking context and will be shown in a separate column:

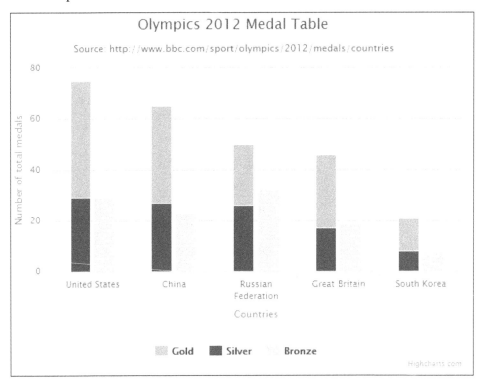

In the next example, we will configure the column chart to stack data series proportionally for each category.

Drilling down the chart

Consider the following table showing the retail revenue breakdown by month for the US video game industry starting from March 2012 to February 2014:

	Mar	Apr	May	Jun	Jul	Aug	Sep	Oct	Nov	Dec	Jan	Feb
2012 - 2013	1.1	0.63	0.52	0.7	0.55	0.52	0.85	0.76	2.55	3.21	0.84	0.81
2013 - 2014	0.99	0.5	0.39	0.59	0.44	0.52	1.08	0.79	2.74	3.28	0.66	0.89

This table shows the revenue (in billions of US dollars) for the video game retail industry. In this example, we will plot a chart to visualize this data. We will draw a column chart that shows the total revenue for the fiscal year starting from March 2012 to February 2014. On clicking on the column, the reader will be shown a more detailed column chart showing the breakdown by months for the respective year.

To use the drilldown feature, you need to include the `Highcharts-4.x.x/js/modules/drilldown.js` file in your HTML after the `Highcharts.js` file. Not doing so will not throw any error or warning, but the drilldown feature will not work, hence making debugging difficult.

To start creating the drilldown chart for the table data, perform the following steps:

1. Create a new blank HTML file and paste in the following code:

```
<!doctype html>
<html lang="en">
<head>
  <meta charset="UTF-8">
  <title>Highcharts Essentials</title>
</head>
<body>

  <div id="revenue_chart" style="width: 600px;
    height: 450px;"></div>

  <script src="http://ajax.googleapis.com/ajax/libs/jquery/1.11.1/
  jquery.min.js"></script>
  <script src="js/highcharts.js"></script>
  <script src="js/modules/drilldown.js"></script>
</body>
</html>
```

2. Let's first draw a column chart to display the total yearly revenue:

```
(function() {
  $( '#revenue_chart' ).highcharts({
    chart: {
      type: 'column'
    },
    title: {
      text: 'Retail Revenue for Video Game Industry'
    },
    subtitle: {
      text: 'Source: NPD Group; AFJV'
    },
    xAxis: {
      title: {
        text: 'Years'
      },
      Type: 'category'
    },
    yAxis: {
      title: {
        text: 'Revenue (in U.S. billion dollars)'
      }
    },
    series: [{
      data: [{
        name: '2012 - 2013',
        y: 13.04
      }, {
        name: '2013 - 2014',
        y: 12.87
      }]
    }]
  });
})();
```

In the preceding code, we passed the data series for each category as a distinct data object that includes the name of the data series and its value on the *y* axis. The preceding code will produce the following chart:

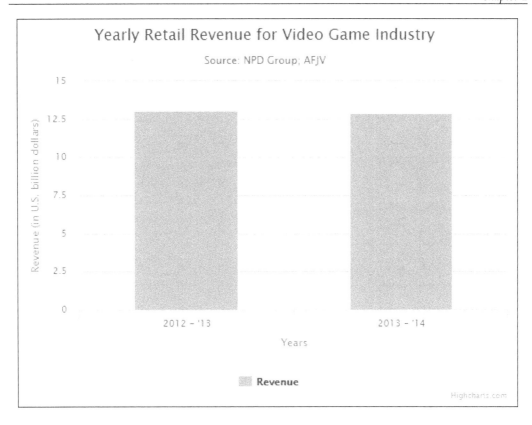

To enable the drilldown feature, we will specify the IDs of the drilldown series to be used for both categories (years) and then pass those series as a data object in the drilldown component:

1. Modify your series component to reference the IDs of the drilldowns to be used as follows:

```
series: [{
  data: [{
    name: '2012 - 2013',
    y: 13.04,
    drilldown: 'rev1213'
  }, {
    name: '2013 - 2014',
    y: 12.87,
    drilldown: 'rev1314'
  }]
}]
```

2. Now, include in your code the `drilldown` component:

```
drilldown: {
  series: [{
    name: 'Revenue',
    id: 'rev1213',
    data: [
      ['Mar', 1.1], ['Apr', 0.63], ['May', 0.52],
        ['Jun', 0.7], ['Jul', 0.55], ['Aug', 0.52],
          ['Sep', 0.85], ['Oct', 0.76], ['Nov', 2.55],
            ['Dec', 3.21], ['Jan', 0.84], ['Feb', 0.81]
    ]
  }, {
    name: 'Revenue',
    id: 'rev1314',
    data: [
      ['Mar', 0.99], ['Apr', 0.5], ['May', 0.39],
        ['Jun', 0.59], ['Jul', 0.44], ['Aug', 0.52],
          ['Sep', 1.08], ['Oct', 0.79], ['Nov', 2.74],
            ['Dec', 3.28], ['Jan', 0.66], ['Feb', 0.89]
    ]
  }]
}
```

Notice the `id` properties of the drilldown series that are the same as used to reference in the drilldown parent point.

3. Now, click on any of the columns and you will be taken to another chart showing the revenue breakdown, as shown in the following screenshot:

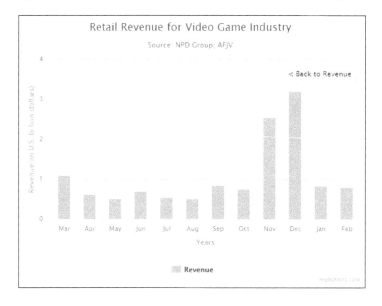

Notice the **Back to Revenue** button that shows up after drilling down into the child chart.

 You can find out more about the Highcharts drilldown feature by visiting the official documentation at `http://api.highcharts.com/highcharts#drilldown`.

Adjusting ticks and other chart elements

We can adjust the interval between the ticks that appear on the *y* axis by using the `tickInterval` property:

1. Modify the `yAxis` component from the previous example to set a difference of 1 between each tick:

```
yAxis: {
  title: {
    text: 'Revenue (in U.S. billion dollars)'
  },
  tickInterval: 1
}
```

2. We can also include HTML in our titles and other text properties by enabling the `useHTML` property. Let's point to the actual data source in our subtitle:

```
subtitle: {
  text: 'Source: <a href="http://www.npd.com"
    title="NPD Group">NPD Group</a>; AFJV',
  useHTML: true
}
```

3. Now, add a bit of CSS styling by using the `style` property:

```
style: {
  color: '#000000',
  textDecoration: 'underline'
}
```

The resulting chart from the previous modification will be like the
following screenshot:

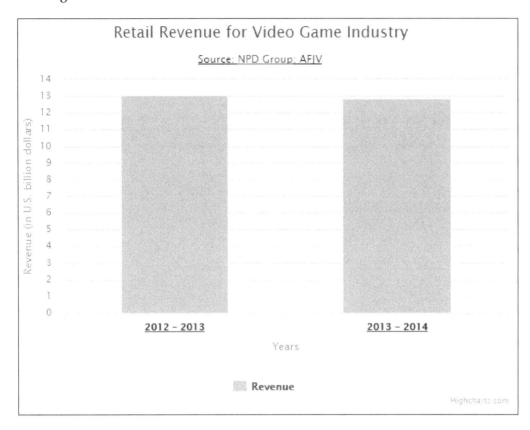

Introducing bar charts

Bar charts are similar to column charts, except that they are aligned vertically.

In the following example, we will create a basic bar chart to show the book
consumption per capita for the year 2014. Let's start with the basic HTML
template we have been using so far:

```
<!doctype html>
<html lang="en">
<head>
  <meta charset="UTF-8">
  <title>Highcharts Essentials</title>
</head>
```

```
<body>

  <div id="book_consumption" style="width: 600px;
    height: 450px;"></div>

<script src="http://ajax.googleapis.com/ajax/libs/jquery/1.11.1/
jquery.min.js"></script>
<script src="js/highcharts.js"></script>
</body>
</html>
```

The code for the chart is as follows:

```
(function() {
  $( '#book_consumption' ).highcharts({
    chart: {
      type: 'bar'
    },
    title: {
      text: 'Average Book Consumption Per Capita'
    },
    subtitle: {
      text: 'Source: Harris Interactive'
    },
    xAxis: {
      categories: ['0', '1-2', '3-5', '6-10', '11-20', '21+']
    },
    yAxis: {
      min:0,
      max: 25,
      tickInterval: 5
    },
    tooltip: {
      enabled: false
    },
    series: [{
      name: '2014',
      data: [16, 17, 18, 13,15, 21]
    }]
  });
})();
```

Notice the use of min and max in yAxis to define the minimum and maximum values. We have also set an interval of 5 using the tickInterval property.

Since the population is measured in percentage in this particular example, it's appropriate to append a % symbol to the labels on the yAxis component using the formatter method, as shown in the following code:

```
yAxis: {
  min:0,
  max: 25,
  tickInterval: 5,
  labels: {
      enabled: true,
      formatter: function() {
          return this.value + "%";
      }
    }
}
```

This will result in the following chart:

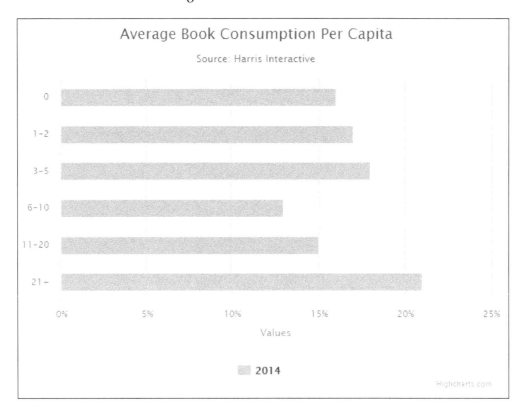

We can also enable `dataLabels` in the `plotOptions` component to show data point values next to the bars:

```
plotOptions: {
  series: {
    dataLabels: {
      enabled: true,
      formatter: function() {
        return this.y + '%';
      }
    }
  }
}
```

We used the `formatter` method to append a `%` symbol next to the values. Also, note that we referenced the data point values using `this.y` inside the formatter.

The data labels will now appear next to the bars, as shown in the following screenshot:

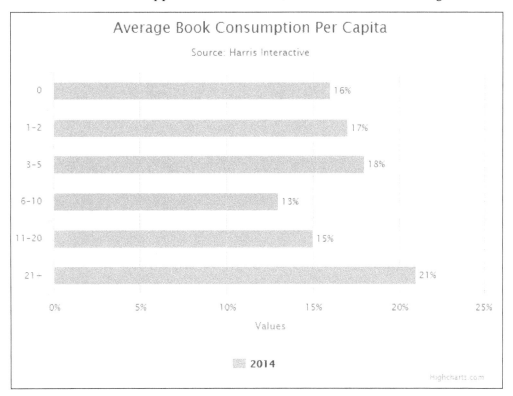

You might also be interested in other properties that are available in the formatter() method. You can find more about them at http://api.highcharts.com/highcharts#tooltip.formatter.

Negatively stacked bar charts

In this example, we will compare the average book consumption data for the year 2014 with the year 2012 using negative stacking. Copy the code from the previous example and include the data series for the year 2012, as shown in the following code:

```
series: [{
  name: '2014',
  data: [16, 17, 18, 13,15, 21]
}, {
  name: '2012',
  data: [-14, -15, -19, -19, -14, -19]
}]
```

To enable negative stacking, the data series must contain values in negative. We can now enable the stacking in the plotOptions component, as shown in the following code:

```
plotOptions: {
  series: {
    dataLabels: {
      enabled: true,
      formatter: function() {
        return this.y + '%';
      }
    },
    stacking: 'normal'
  }
}
```

However, the negatively stacked bars won't show until we change the min property in yAxis from 0 to -25.

Refresh the page and you should see a negatively stacked bar chart, as shown in the following screenshot:

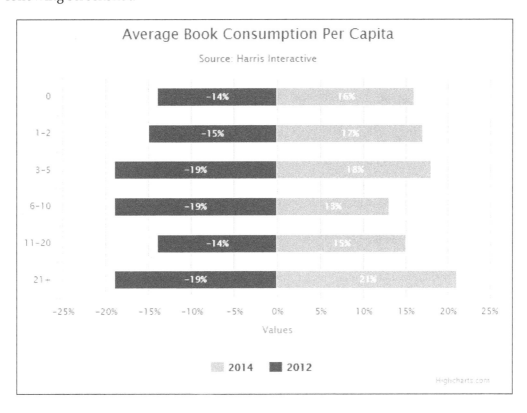

Creating 3D column charts

Along with many new features, Highcharts 4 comes with a long-awaited feature of creating 3D charts. With the new 3D module, column, pie, and scatter charts now support the 3D view. This module enables us to define various properties for the 3D view including the rotation axes and depths.

 In order to plot 3D charts, you need to include the 3D module, `highcharts-4.x.x/js/highcharts-3d.js`, into your page after the main `highcharts.js` file.

Consider the first example from this chapter in which we plotted the data of the London Olympics 2012 medal table showing the medal count of the highest-achieving countries. We will copy the same code and modify `chart.options3d` along with `plotOptions.column` to set up the 3D view:

```
hart: {
    type: 'column',
    options3d: {
        enabled: true,
        alpha: 20,
        beta: 25
    }
}
```

First, we enabled the 3D view in `options3d`. Then, we define the angles at which the chart will be viewed. The `alpha` property is the vertical rotation, while `beta` is the horizontal rotation. Both these properties accept numbers as their values and both have a default value of `0`.

The preceding modification will create a 3D look as follows:

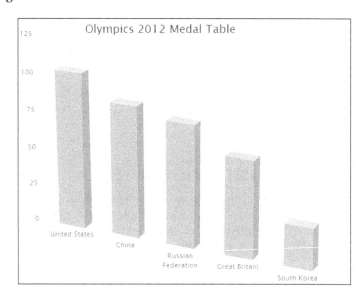

The depth properties control the depth of the chart as well as the columns along the *z* axis. These depth properties can be defined on `options3d` and `plotOptions.column`. In conjunction with these properties, column charts can also be given the `plotOptions.column.groupZPadding` property that controls the distance between the outer edge of the chart and the column groups. The default values of the `options3d.depth` and `plotOptions.column.depth` properties are `100` and `25`, respectively.

Let's modify the `plotOptions` component and the `options3d` object literal to see how the previously mentioned properties work:

```
chart: {
  type: 'column',
  options3d: {
    enabled: true,
    alpha: 20,
    beta: 25,
    depth: 120
  }
},
plotOptions: {
  column: {
    depth: 50,
    groupZPadding: 50
  }
}
}
```

Modifying the values of `plotOptions.column.depth` and `options3d.depth` to be larger than their default values caused the depths of the columns and the chart to increase. The default value of `plotOptions.column.groupZPadding` is 0, which aligns the columns with the outer edge of the chart. However, increasing its value pushed the columns inwards into the chart along the *z* axis.

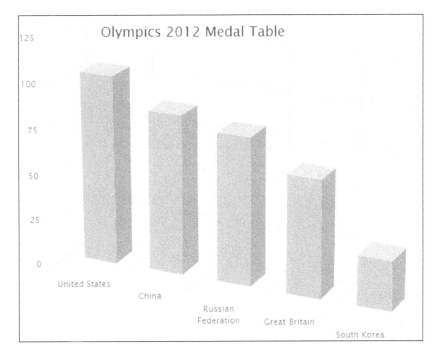

Likewise, column charts with multiple series and stacking can also incorporate the 3D view. The following screenshot of two 3D charts is produced by customizing the code of the previous examples of this chapter. You can find the full code in the accompanying code examples of this book:

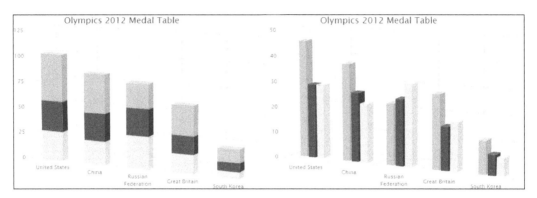

Modifying the viewing frame

Highcharts also allows us to modify the viewing frame of a 3D chart. This includes customizing the back, bottom, and side panels of the virtual box in which the 3D chart is present. We can do so by accessing `options3d.frame` as well as the `side`, `bottom`, and `back` properties:

```
frame: {
  back: {
    color: '#c2dbf2',
    size: 5
  },
  bottom: {
    color: '#adc4d9',
    size: 5
  },
  side: {
    color: '#b8cfe5',
    size: 5
  }
}
```

This code will modify the look of the view box, as shown in the following screenshot:

The `size` property controls the thickness, while the `color` property determines the color of its respective panel.

> To learn more about the 3D features of Highcharts, check out the official documentation at `http://api.highcharts.com/highcharts#chart.options3d`.

Summary

In this chapter, we took a detailed look at column and bar charts. We learned about various configuration options to alter the look and feel of the charts and also using the Highcharts API to format certain chart elements. Introducing these basic concepts, this chapter should have given you a fairly solid base to get started with Highcharts development.

In the next chapter, you will learn about the line and spline chart types. We will begin by creating some basic charts as well as loading data from a HTML table and configuring charts with inverted axes.

3
Line and Spline Charts

In the previous chapter, you learned about two common chart types: column charts and bar charts. In this chapter, we will explore two other common chart types: line charts and spline charts.

In this chapter, you will learn how to:

- Create line charts with regular time intervals
- Format the date and time
- Format data labels and the tooltip
- Create line charts with irregular time intervals
- Create line charts with multiple series
- Load data to be plotted from within an HMTL table
- Create spline charts
- Create spline charts with plot bands
- Combine line and column charts

Introducing line charts

Line charts show a series of data points connected by a straight line. They often show a set of data in which the quantity varies over time, or data that has any sort of sequential steps. Thus, they help to find trends in data series that enable us to forecast the future behavior of the quantity.

When talking about time-dependent series, there are two types:

- Series with regular time intervals
- Series with irregular time intervals

In the following examples, we will have a look at plotting both types of series with line charts.

Creating line charts with regular time intervals

In the following example, we will plot a line chart for hourly temperature data for Pittsburgh, PA, for January 1, 2013.

Since we are dealing with the date/time series with regular time intervals, we will declare the `type` property of `xAxis` to be `datetime`, and while passing the `pointStart` and `pointInterval` properties to the series, we can easily plot the data mentioned.

Let's start with our basic HTML template containing the following code:

```
<!doctype html>
<html lang="en">
<head>
  <meta charset="UTF-8">
  <title>Highcharts Essentials</title>
</head>
<body>

  <div id="chart_container" style="width: 600px;
    height: 450px;"></div>

<script src="http://ajax.googleapis.com/ajax/libs/jquery/1.11.1/
jquery.min.js"></script>
<script src="js/highcharts.js"></script>
</body>
</html>
```

 Please note that for all the upcoming examples in this book, we will use the same HTML template to kick-start our coding process unless mentioned otherwise.

Now, paste the following JavaScript code in the preceding HTML template to render the chart. We will examine it bit by bit in a moment:

```
(function() {
  $( '#chart_container' ).highcharts({
    chart: {
```

```
        type: 'line'
    },
    title: {
        text: 'Hourly Temperature Data for Pittsburgh, PA'
    },
    subtitle: {
        text: 'Source: <a href="http://www.noaa.gov/"> National Weather
Service Forecast Office</a>',
        useHTML: true
    },
    xAxis: {
        type: 'datetime'
    },
    yAxis: {
        title: {
            text: 'Temperature (&deg;F)',
            useHTML: true
        }
    },
    series: [{
        name: 'Temperature',
        pointStart: Date.UTC(2013, 00, 01, 00, 00, 00),
        pointInterval: 3600 * 1000,
        data: [32, 32, 31, 31, 31, 31, 31, 31, 31, 31, 31, 31, 30, 30,
30, 30, 28, 27, 27, 26, 25, 24, 23, 22]
    }]
    });
})();
```

In the preceding code, we first declared the `type` property of the `xAxis` to be
`datetime`. This allows us to mention the number of milliseconds in order to set
the starting point and the time interval. Highcharts then displays the appropriate
format of the date/time on the axes.

The `Date.UTC()` method used in the series component is the native JavaScript method
that takes in the date/time and returns the Unix timestamp, that is, the number of
milliseconds elapsed since the midnight of January 1, 1970. The parameters passed
are for year, month, day, hour, minutes, and seconds respectively.

 The months in UTC time format are represented by an integer ranging
from 0 to 11. So January is represented by 0, February by 1, and
December by 11.

Since we needed to plot the data on an hourly basis, we set `pointInterval` to `3600 * 1000`, that is, the number of milliseconds in an hour.

The previous code will produce the following line chart:

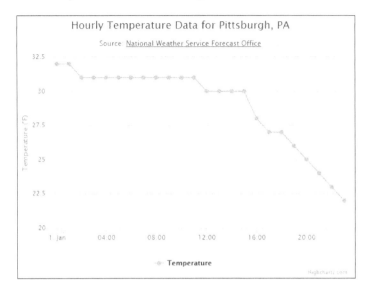

In the next step, we will format the date/time on the *x* axis.

Formatting date/time and data labels

Currently, the chart is displaying the hours on the *x* axis with an interval of four hours. We can modify it by passing the number of milliseconds for *x* number of hours for the `tickInterval` property of the `xAxis` component:

```
xAxis: {
  type: 'datetime',
  tickInterval: 3600 * 1000 * 3
}
```

Hence, we modified the `tickInterval` property to be 3 hours instead of 4:

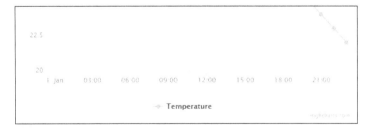

You can find more about the `tickInterval` property at `http://api.highcharts.com/highcharts#xAxis.tickInterval`.

You might have noticed that the first data label on the *x* axis is being interpreted as a day instead of an hour. We can fix it by overriding the default values of `dateTimeLabelFormats`. The `dateTimeLabelFormats` object allows us to format the date and time for a number of components of Highcharts. The default values are as follows:

```
{
    millisecond:"%A, %b %e, %H:%M:%S.%L",
    second:"%A, %b %e, %H:%M:%S",
    minute:"%A, %b %e, %H:%M",
    hour:"%A, %b %e, %H:%M",
    day:"%A, %b %e, %Y",
    week:"Week from %A, %b %e, %Y",
    month:"%b'%y",
    year:"%Y"
}
```

We will change the `day` property to be the same as the `hour` property:

```
dateTimeLabelFormats: {
    day: '%H:%M'
}
```

Adding the preceding code to the `xAxis` component, we will get the following result:

```
22.5

20
    00:00    03:00    06:00    09:00    12:00    15:00    18:00    21:00

              ─── Temperature

                                                      Highcharts.com
```

We can also change the 24-hour time format to the 12-hour format by modifying the `hour` property:

```
dateTimeLabelFormats: {
    day: '%I:%M',
    hour: '%I:%M'
}
```

Changing the format will give the following result:

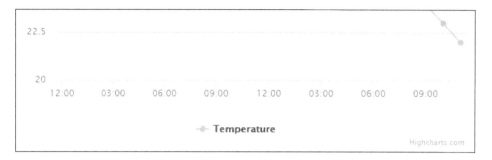

It's more appropriate to show A.M. or P.M. with the 12-hour format. We can do it as shown in the following code:

```
dateTimeLabelFormats: {
    day: '%I %p',
    hour: '%I %p'
}
```

The result of this modification will be as follows:

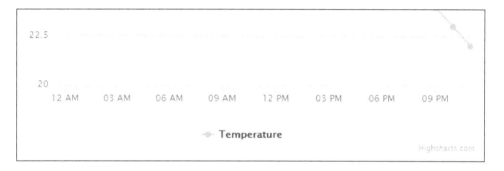

Formatting the tooltip

Currently, the tooltip is not very helpful when trying to understand the relation between time and temperature.

We need to modify the tooltip to say something like **The temperature at 6 AM was 32 °F.**

We can achieve this result by using the `formatter()` method that Highcharts provides to format labels and tooltips.

Insert the following code for the tooltip component:

```
tooltip: {
  formatter: function() {
     return 'The temperature at ' + this.x + ' was ' + this.y + '
&deg;F'
  },
  useHTML: true
}
```

Here we referenced the date on `xAxis` by using `this.x` and the temperature by using `this.y`.

The tooltip is now formatted to display the following:

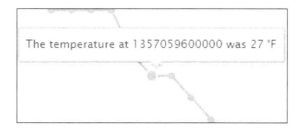

We still need to format the time to show the hour instead of the number of milliseconds. For this purpose, we will use the `Highcharts.dateFormat()` method that takes in the string format and the JavaScript date timestamp to produce a human-readable date format.

Modify the `formatter()` method to include the `Highcharts.dateFormat()` function:

```
formatter: function() {
  return 'The temperature at ' + Highcharts.dateFormat('%I %p',
this.x) + ' was ' + this.y + ' &deg;F'
}
```

The tooltip will now show the proper time of day:

So far, we have covered how to create line charts with regular time intervals, format the date/time with the help of various properties and methods that Highcharts provides, and finally format the tooltip to show data specific to our requirements. In the next example, we will look at creating line charts with irregular time intervals.

Creating line charts with irregular time intervals

The main difference between line charts with irregular time intervals and those with regular time intervals is that the latter has a fixed point interval. The problem with the charts with irregular intervals is that we can't define a single point interval, hence we have to manually provide the date/time against each data point in the series.

Consider the example of conversion rates of USD to Euros at the end of each month. Months fall in the category of irregular time intervals because each month can be 28 (leap year), 29, 30, or 31 days.

In the following example, we will create a line chart with irregular time intervals (months) to analyze the conversion rate of Euros to US Dollars for a period of 7 months starting from September 2013 to March 2014:

```
(function() {
  $( '#chart_container' ).highcharts({
    chart: {
      type: 'line'
    },
    title: {
      text: 'Historical Conversion Rates of Euro to USD'
    },
    subtitle: {
      text: 'Source: <a href="http://www.oanda.com/">www.oanda.com</
a>',
      useHTML: true
    },
    xAxis: {
```

```
        type: 'datetime'
      },
      yAxis: {
        title: {
          text: 'USD'
        }
      },
      series: [{
        name: 'Euro',
        data: [
          [Date.UTC(2013, 08, 01), 1.3343],
          [Date.UTC(2013, 09, 01), 1.3634],
          [Date.UTC(2013, 10, 01), 1.3694],
          [Date.UTC(2013, 11, 01), 1.3633],
          [Date.UTC(2014, 00, 01), 1.3644],
          [Date.UTC(2014, 01, 01), 1.3825],
          [Date.UTC(2014, 02, 01), 1.3806]
        ]
      }]
    });
  })();
```

Here, we passed the first of each month in the Unix timestamp against each date point using the `Date.UTC()` method, which we learned in the earlier examples. This will produce the following chart:

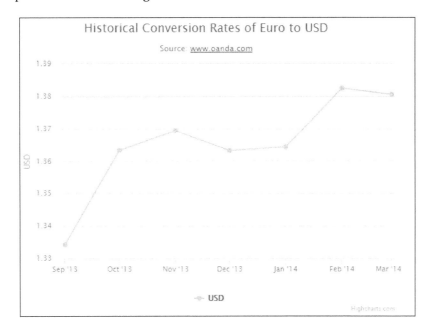

Let's quickly format the tooltip using the `formatter()` function:

```
tooltip: {
  formatter: function() {
    var string = Highcharts.dateFormat( '%b\'%y', this.x ) + '<br>';
    string += '1 Euro = ' + this.y + ' USD';
    return string;
  },
  useHTML: true
}
```

By using the `formatter()` function, we will get the following result:

The tooltip is now formatted to show the conversion rates of both currencies along with their units.

Creating line charts with multiple series

We can also create a line chart with multiple series just as we did with column charts in the previous chapter. We will also include the conversion rates of GBP in our chart along with USD and Euro.

Copy the code from the previous example and add a series for GBP:

```
{
  name: 'GBP',
  data: [
    [Date.UTC(2013, 08, 01), 1.5835],
    [Date.UTC(2013, 09, 01), 1.6092],
    [Date.UTC(2013, 10, 01), 1.6088],
    [Date.UTC(2013, 11, 01), 1.6368],
    [Date.UTC(2014, 00, 01), 1.6468],
    [Date.UTC(2014, 01, 01), 1.6546],
    [Date.UTC(2014, 02, 01), 1.6629]
  ]
}
```

Refresh the page and the series for GBP will now be included in the chart.

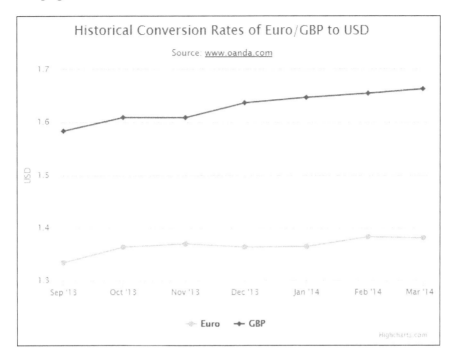

There is one problem though: if you hover over any data point of the GBP series, the tooltip will keep mentioning Euro instead of GBP:

This is because we hardcoded the series name as Euro in our tooltip's `formatter()` method. Change it to the following and the tooltip will start working correctly:

```
formatter: function() {
  var string = Highcharts.dateFormat( '%b\'%y', this.x ) + '<br>';
  string += '1 ' + this.series.name + ' = ' + this.y + ' USD';
  return string;
}
```

So instead of referencing the series name manually, we referenced it by using the `this.series.name` property that will return the name of the series currently hovered over:

The tooltip now shows the conversion rate of both currencies with their respective units.

Loading data from an HTML table

So far in this book, we have looked at drawing charts by manually providing data in the form of a series. However, we can actually go beyond this default functionality and load the data to be plotted in various ways. HTML tables are commonly used to mark up data for web pages, and Highcharts provides us with a functionality to load data right from HTML tables instead of passing it in the series component.

 The data module is required in order to be able to load the data directly from the HTML table. You can find it at `Highcharts-4.x.x/js/modules/data.js`.

Consider the following HTML table code with an ID of `vehicle_data` that shows the number of cars and commercial vehicles manufactured in the UK from 2008 to 2012:

```
<table id="vehicle_data">
  <thead>
    <tr>
      <th></th>
      <th>Cars</th>
      <th>Commercial Vehicles</th>
    </tr>
  </thead>
  <tbody>
    <tr>
      <th>2008</th>
      <td>1446619</td>
      <td>202896</td>
    </tr>
```

```
    <tr>
      <th>2009</th>
      <td>999460</td>
      <td>90679</td>
    </tr>
    <tr>
      <th>2010</th>
      <td>1270444</td>
      <td>123019</td>
    </tr>
    <tr>
      <th>2011</th>
      <td>1343810</td>
      <td>120189</td>
    </tr>
    <tr>
      <th>2012</th>
      <td>1464906</td>
      <td>112039</td>
    </tr>
  </tbody>
</table>
```

We also need to include the data module after the `highcharts.js` script, as shown in the following code:

```
<script src="Highcharts4.x.x/js/highcharts.js"></script>
<script src=" Highcharts4.x.x/js/modules/data.js"></script>
```

The JavaScript code to plot the chart is as follows:

```
(function() {

  $( '#chart_container' ).highcharts({
    chart: {
      type: 'line'
    },
    title: {
      text: 'Vehicles Manufactured in the UK'
    },
    subtitle: {
      text: 'Source: <a href="http://www.oica.net/">OICA</a>',
      useHTML: true
    },
    data: {
```

```
        table: document.getElementById( 'vehicle_data' )
    }
  });

}) ();
```

This will produce the following line chart showing the data:

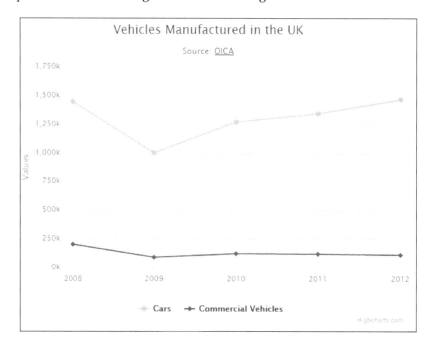

You can add as many data series to the HTML table as you want to plot the data.

Creating spline charts

Spline charts are similar to line charts; the only difference is that in line charts, the data points are connected by a straight line whereas in spline charts, the points are connected by curves. A line chart can easily be converted into a spline chart by changing the chart type from line to spline.

Consider the following example showing **Producer Price Index (PPI)** in the US from 2007 to 2012:

```
(function() {
  $( '#chart_container' ).highcharts({
    chart: {
      type: 'spline'
```

```
        },

        title: {
          text: 'Producer Price Index (PPI) in the US'
        },
        subtitle: {
          text: 'Source: Bureau of Labor Statistics'
        },
        xAxis: {
          type: 'datetime'
        },
        series: [{
          name: 'PPI',
          data: [
            [Date.UTC(2007, 00, 01), 172.6],
            [Date.UTC(2008, 00, 01), 189.6],
            [Date.UTC(2009, 00, 01), 172.9],
            [Date.UTC(2010, 00, 01), 184.7],
            [Date.UTC(2011, 00, 01), 201],
            [Date.UTC(2012, 00, 01), 202.2]
          ]
        }]
      });
    })();
```

This code will result in the following spline chart:

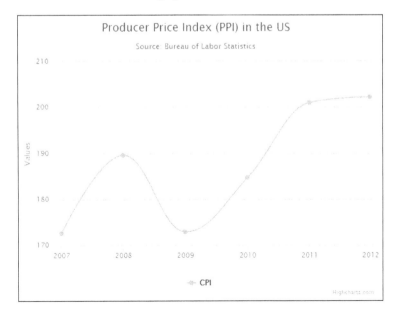

Creating spline charts with plot bands

Plot bands are yet another feature of Highcharts that greatly improve the visualization of the data. They are always perpendicular to the axis in which they are defined.

Considering the previous example, we will insert two plot bands in the yAxis component of our chart:

- **Low**: This is for the PPI below and equal to 200
- **High**: This is for the PPI above the 200 mark

Include the following code in the previous example for the yAxis component:

```
yAxis: {
  plotBands: [{
    from: 0,
    to: 200,
    color: 'rgba(82, 174, 0, 0.2)',
    label: {
      text: 'Low',
      style: {
        color: 'rgb(82, 174, 0)'
      }
    }
  }, {
    from: 200,
    to: 300,
    color: 'rgba(174, 0, 0, 0.2)',
    label: {
      text: 'High',
      style: {
        color: 'rgb(174, 0, 0)'
      }
    }
  }]
}
```

The following is the screenshot of the resulting chart:

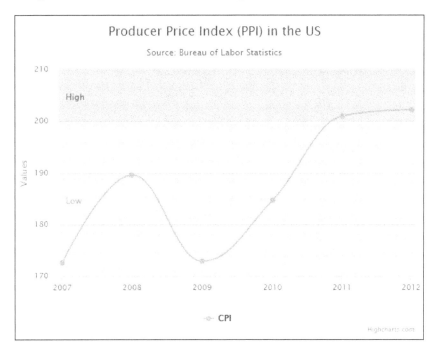

Combining line and column charts

Consider the following example that shows the sales of smartphones to end users in each quarter of the year 2013. For the sake of simplicity, only three leading vendors have been included:

```
(function() {
  $( '#chart_container' ).highcharts({
    title: {
      text: 'Global Smartphone Sales in 2013'
    },
    subtitle: {
      text: 'Source: Gartner'
    },
    xAxis: {
      categories: ["Q1'13", "Q2'13", "Q3'13"]
```

```
      },
      yAxis: {
        title: {
          text: 'Units (in millions)'
        }
      },
      series: [{
        name: 'Android',
        type: 'column',
        data: [156.19, 177.9, 205.02]
      }, {
        name: 'iOS',
        type: 'column',
        data: [38.33, 31.9, 30.33]
      }, {
        name: 'Microsoft',
        type: 'column',
        data: [5.99, 7.41, 8.91]
      }]
    });
  })();
```

This code generates a column chart that consists of three series for Android, iOS, and Microsoft with the numbers of their units sold in millions:

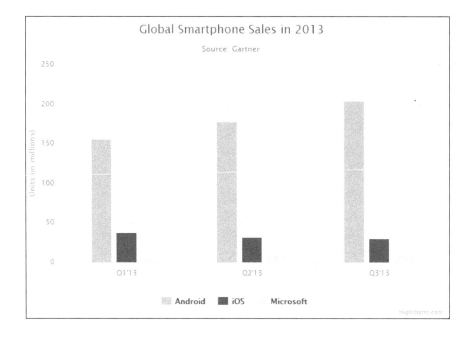

We can easily introduce another series with `type` as `line` to show the total number of sales made in that quarter:

```
{
  name: 'Total',
  type: 'line',
  data: [200.51, 217.21, 244.26]
}
```

The additional series of type line is now inserted in the following chart showing the total number of sales in each quarter:

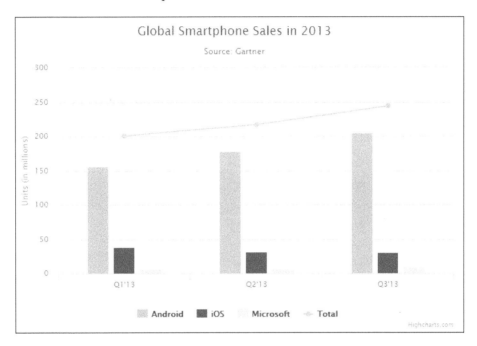

Summary

This concludes our third chapter in which you were introduced to line and spline charts. In this chapter, we learned various techniques to deal with regular and irregular time intervals, formatting dates and times, and customizing tooltips. We also looked at loading the data directly from an HTML table using the data module that Highcharts provides for this purpose. At the end of this chapter, we took a column chart that consisted of multiple series and combined it with a line chart to provide a more robust visual feedback for the data. In the next chapter, we will learn about area, scatter, and bubble chart types along with their properties and methods.

4
Area, Scatter, and Bubble Charts

In this chapter, we will examine the area, scatter, and bubble chart types; their configuration options and their use cases. We will cover the following:

- Creating area and area-spline charts
- Formatting the tooltip in a simpler manner
- Creating scatter charts with single and multiple series
- Creating bubble charts

Introducing area charts

Area charts are similar to line charts but are slightly different in the way that they show colors below the lines. This color-filled area displays quantitative data in a more distinguished manner. Area charts are typically useful for displaying multiple series with large sets of data points.

Consider the following example showing the net income of Microsoft from 2005 to 2013. Due to the relatively large number of data points (that is, 10), it's more appropriate to visualize this data by an area chart instead of a column or bar chart.

```
(function() {
  $( '#chart_container' ).highcharts({
    chart: {
      type: 'area'
    },
    title: {
      text: 'Yearly Net Income of Microsoft'
    },
```

```
    subtitle: {
      text: 'Source: Microsoft'
    },
    xAxis: {
      categories:
        [2005, 2006, 2007, 2008, 2009, 2010, 2011, 2012, 2013]
    },
    yAxis: {
      title: {
        text: 'Revenue in billion USD'
      }
    },
    series: [{
      name: 'Microsoft',
      data: [12.25, 12.6, 14.07, 17.68, 14.57, 18.76, 23.15,
        16.98, 21.86]
    }]
  });
}) ();
```

We rendered an area chart by setting the type property of the chart to area. The following is the screenshot of the resulting chart:

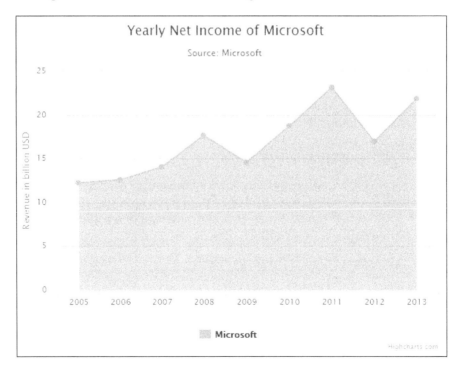

Adjusting the placement of tick marks

If you have a keen eye, you might have noticed that the tick marks on the *x* axis do not appear at the center of each category but rather they appear between the categories, as shown in the following screenshot:

We can correct this issue by passing the `tickmarkPlacement` property of the `xAxis` component with the value `on`:

```
xAxis: {
  tickmarkPlacement: 'on',
  categories:
    [2005, 2006, 2007, 2008, 2009, 2010, 2011, 2012, 2013]
}
```

The tick marks will now appear at the center of each category corresponding to the data points, as shown in the following screenshot:

Eager to learn more about the `tickmarkPlacement` property? Visit the official documentation at `http://api.highcharts.com/highcharts#xAxis.tickmarkPlacement`.

Creating area charts with multiple series

Area charts come in handy when we have data comprising multiple series. By plotting the multiple series data with an area chart, it becomes simple to compare each data point of a series with that of another series while also observing the trend that's being shown by the data.

Configure the chart from the previous example to include another series showing the net income of Apple so we can compare it with Microsoft:

```
series: [{
  name: 'Microsoft',
  data:
    [12.25, 12.6, 14.07, 17.68, 14.57, 18.76, 23.15, 16.98, 21.86]
}, {
  name: 'Apple',
  data: [1.33, 1.99, 3.5, 6.12, 8.24, 14.01, 25.92, 41.73, 37.04]
}]
```

The following screenshot shows the area chart with two series for Microsoft and Apple that will be rendered with the preceding code:

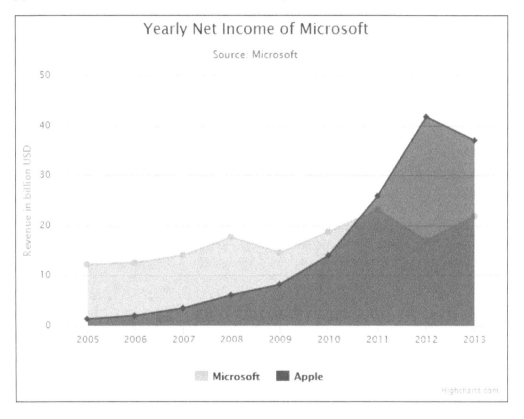

Highcharts shows multiple series in an area chart with semitransparent colors. This makes it easy to view data points behind other series that would be hidden otherwise.

Series with missing values

Suppose that at one point in the Apple series we are not provided with data values. In that case, we can pass `null` in place of missing values and Highcharts will automatically adjust the chart:

```
{
  name: 'Apple',
  data: [1.33, 1.99, 3.5, null, null, 14.01, 25.92, 41.73, 37.04]
}
```

This will break the series where `null` is provided.

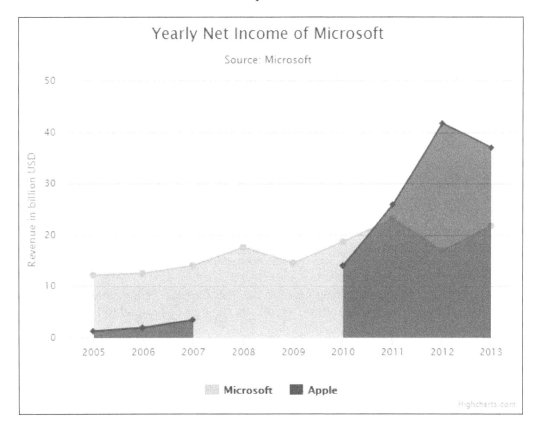

Sharing a tooltip between multiple series

Sharing the tooltip between data points of multiple series makes it convenient when comparing large amount of data. It enables us to compare a data point of a series with corresponding data points of other series by simply hovering over a single data point.

We can enable the shared tooltip in the chart from the previous example by modifying the tooltip component, as shown in the following code:

```
tooltip: {
   shared: true
}
```

Hover over any data point and a tooltip will appear showing the values of the corresponding data points of other series, as shown in the following screenshot:

At this point, this tooltip adds even more to the user experience and interactivity by incorporating the `crosshair` tooltip that follows the cursor parallel to the *y* axis, as someone hovers over the data points:

```
tooltip: {
   shared: true,
   crosshairs: {
      width: 1,
      color: '#333333',
      dashStyle: 'shortdot'
   }
}
```

The `crosshair` tooltip will look like the following:

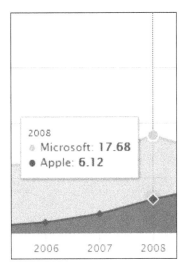

Stacking charts with multiple series

By stacking the area charts, one can easily compare the series in a proportional or total format. Stacking can be applied to all or some of the series in the charts.

Consider the following data of the past 4 years showing the production of iron ore by major mining countries:

```
(function() {
  $( '#chart_container' ).highcharts({
    chart: {
      type: 'area'
    },
    title: {
      text: 'Iron Ore Production'
    },
    xAxis: {
      tickmarkPlacement: 'on',
      categories: [2010, 2011, 2012, 2013]
    },
    yAxis: {
      title: {
        text: 'in million metric tons'
      }
```

```
    },
    series: [{
      name: 'China',
      data: [1070, 1330, 1310, 1320]
    }, {
      name: 'Australia',
      data: [433, 488, 521, 530]
    }, {
      name: 'Brazil',
      data: [370, 373, 398, 398]
    }, {
      name: 'India',
      data: [230, 240, 144, 150]
    }, {
      name: 'Russia',
      data: [101, 100, 105, 102]
    }]
  });
})();
```

This code will produce the following area chart with four series. Though not stacked at the moment, it simply shows how area charts can visualize quantitative data with multiple series:

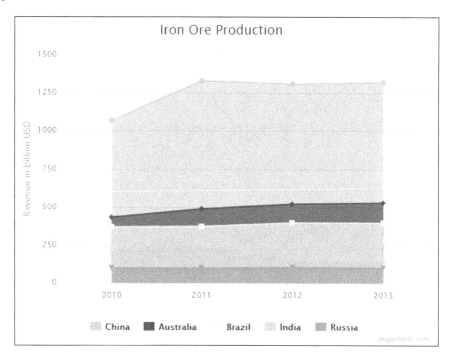

To turn on the stacking, we need to modify the `plotOptions` component as shown in the following code; we tackled the same component in *Chapter 2, Column and Bar Charts*:

```
plotOptions: {
  area: {
    stacking: 'normal'
  }
}
```

This modification of the `plotOptions` component will cause the series in the chart to stack on top of each other, as shown in the following screenshot:

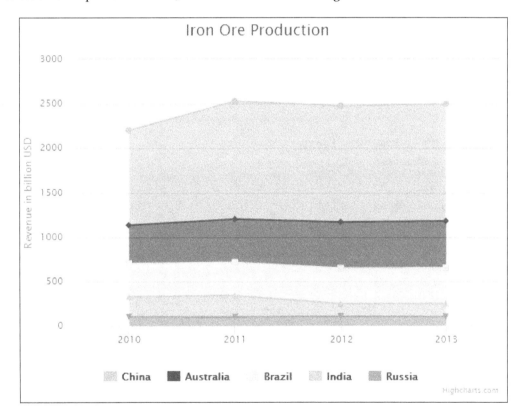

Polishing the area chart

Highcharts allows us to modify the color and opacity of an individual series by passing a color value in the `color` property.

Modify the series to have custom colors for their components:

```
series: [{
  name: 'China',
  data: [1070, 1330, 1310, 1320],
  color: '#d62f2f'
}, {
  name: 'Australia',
  data: [433, 488, 521, 530],
  color: '#1347f0'
}, {
  name: 'Brazil',
  data: [370, 373, 398, 398],
  color: '#4b8303'
}, {
  name: 'India',
  data: [230, 240, 144, 150],
  color: '#d0710b'
}, {
  name: 'Russia',
  data: [101, 100, 105, 102],
  color: '#6b1bef'
}]
```

Doing so will change the colors of the series from default presets to the values provided:

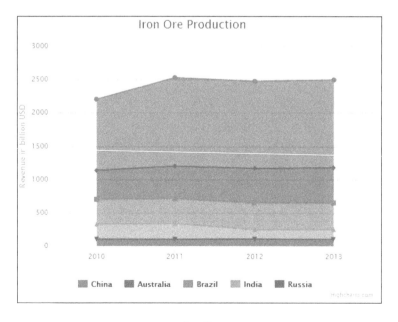

Setting the `color` property changes the color of all the components of the series, including the fill area and line. To set different colors to area and line, use the `fillColor` and `lineColor` properties on individual series, as shown in the following code:

```
{
    name: 'China',
    data: [1070, 1330, 1310, 1320],
    color: '#f25555',
    fillColor: '#d62f2f',
    lineColor: '#a62424'
}
```

The preceding code will cause the `China` series to have different colors for the area, line, and other components, as shown in the following screenshot:

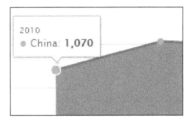

We can also change the opacity of individual series by passing a value from 0 to 1 to the `fillOpacity` property. This feature comes in handy when you want to display data points behind other series in nonstacked charts:

```
{
    name: 'China',
    data: [1070, 1330, 1310, 1320],
    color: '#f25555',
    lineColor: '#a62424',
    fillOpacity: 0.25
}
```

This will give the following result:

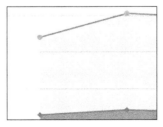

Area charts with percentage values

With percentage stacking, an area chart fills all of the vertical space available with its series sized in a proportional manner. Area charts with percentage stacking can be configured by setting `stacking` to `percent` in the `plotOptions` component:

```
plotOptions: {
  area: {
    stacking: 'percent'
  }
}
```

This code will produce the following proportional-stacked area chart:

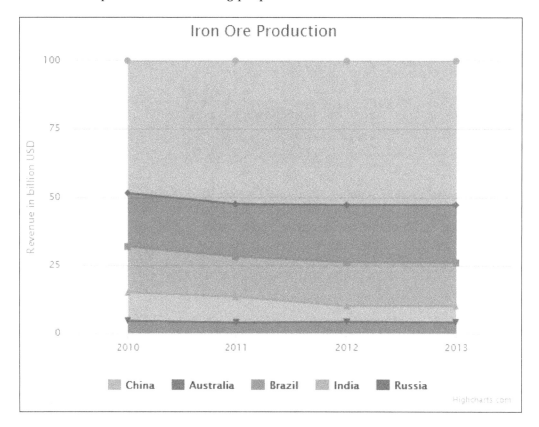

Area-spline charts

Area-spline charts are similar to area charts; however, as the name suggests, they are based on spline charts. Since all the configuration options for area-spline charts are identical to that of area charts, we can easily interchange the two chart types.

Consider the code from the very first example in this chapter, where we visualized the net income of Microsoft and Apple, and change the chart's `type` parameter from `area` to `areaspline`:

```
chart: {
  type: 'areaspline'
}
```

This will change the chart to area-spline:

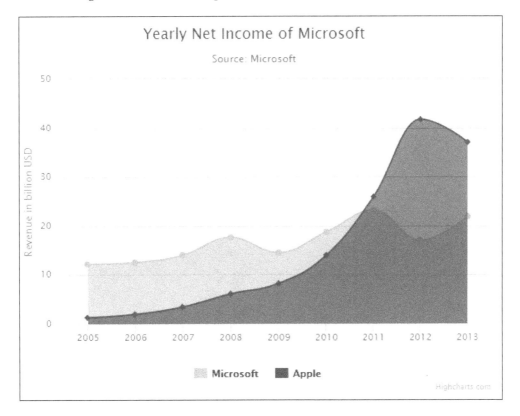

Introducing scatter charts

Scatter charts are different from line and area charts in the way that they don't require sorting. This means that data can be provided in the series with each data point as an array of coordinates, including the values of the *x* and *y* axes in any order.

Consider the following scatter showing the relation between magnitude and depth of earthquakes in Calexico, California during the year 2010:

```
$( '#chart_container' ).highcharts({
  chart: {
    type: 'scatter'
  },
  title: {
    text: 'Earthquake Statistics'
  },
  subtitle: {
    text: 'Data Source: <a href="http://www.scsn.
org/2010sierraelmayor.html">SCSN</a>'
  },
  xAxis: {
    title: {
      text: 'Depth'
    }
  },
  yAxis: {
    title: {
      text: 'Magnitude'
    },
    min: 3
  },
  tooltip: {
    pointFormat: 'Depth: <strong>{point.x} Km</strong> <br/>Magnitude:
<strong>{point.y}</strong>'
  },
  series: [{
    name: 'Calexico',
    data: [[10, 4.8], [22.6, 4.2], [6, 4.3], [10, 4.2], [10, 4.0],
[5.6, 4.0], [10, 4.0], [10, 4.0], [10, 7.2], [10, 5.5], [10, 5.4],
[10, 5.4], [10, 5.3], [10, 4.8], [10, 4.7], [10, 4.7], [6, 4.6], [10,
4.6], [10, 4.5], [10, 4.5], [10, 4.5]]
  }]
});
```

Notice the way in which data points have been provided in the form of arrays with the *x* value representing the depth and the *y* value representing the magnitude of the earthquake.

The previous code will produce the following scatter chart:

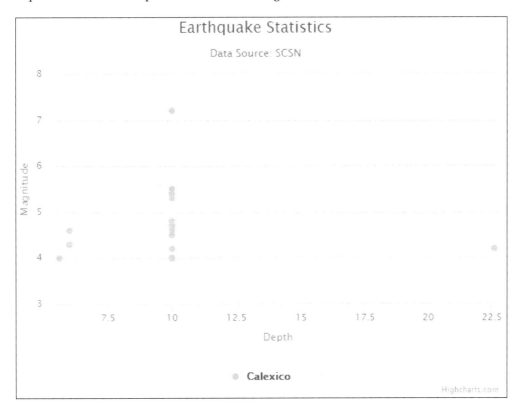

Notice the way in which data is scattered on the whole chart in all directions.

Formatting a tooltip with pointFormat

In *Chapter 3*, *Line and Spline Charts*, we learned about formatting the tooltip using the `formatter()` method. Although the `formatter()` method is really powerful in modifying tooltips with custom markup, there's actually an easy way too: using the `pointFormat` property.

The `pointFormat` property comes in handy when just a little customization is required for the point line. Currently, the tooltip looks like this:

Insert the code for the `tooltip` component as follows:

```
tooltip: {
  pointFormat: 'Depth: <strong>{point.x} Km</strong> <br />Magnitude:
<strong>{point.y}</strong>'
}
```

The available properties inside `pointFormat` are `point.x`, `point.y`, `series.name`, and `series.color`. These properties are enclosed by curly braces.

The preceding code will produce the following customized tooltip:

The customized tooltip shows the **Depth** and **Magnitude** values.

Scatter charts with multiple series

Just as with any other chart type you have learned so far, scatter charts can also be plotted with multiple series.

Copy the code from the previous example and add another series for earthquake data for Ocotillo, California:

```
{
  name: 'Ocotillo',
  data: [[0.1, 5.0], [4.6, 4.6], [4.4, 4.6], [2.3, 4.5], [10, 4.4],
[10, 4.2], [4.9, 4.0], [0.4, 4.5], [13.6, 4.9], [14.4, 4.8], [0, 4.7],
[3, 4.6], [6, 4.6], [1.2, 4.5], [6.8, 4.5], [12.6, 4.4], [5.6, 4.4],
[10, 4.2], [1, 4.1], [0.5, 4.0], [14.1, 4.0]]
}
```

The series for Ocotillo will be added to the previous chart.

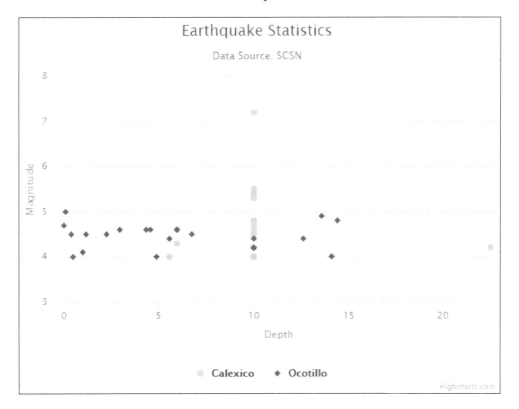

Creating bubble charts

The difference between bubble charts and all the other chart types we have been through is that a bubble chart uses three dimensional data to plot its data point. Hence, instead of providing values for just the x and y axes, we also provide the z axis value as the third variable. Thus, bubble charts can be used for visualizing 3D data where three variables are correlated.

 For the following code to work, you need to include `Highcharts-4.x.x/js/highcharts-more.js` in your page.

Consider the following example in which we plot a bubble chart to show the correlation between life expectancy, fertility rate, and population of selected countries of the world:

```
$( '#chart_container' ).highcharts({
  chart: {
    type: 'bubble'
  },
  title: {
    text: 'Life Expectancy, Fertility Rate and Population'
  },
  xAxis: {
    title: {
      text: 'Life Expectancy'
    }
  },
  yAxis: {
    title: {
      text: 'Fertility Rate'
    }
  },
  tooltip: {
    headerFormat: '<b>{point.key}</b><br />',
    pointFormat: 'Life Expectancy: <strong>{point.x} </strong> <br
/>Fertility Rate: <strong>{point.y} </strong> <br />Population:
<strong>{point.z} </strong>'
  },
  series: [{
    name: 'North America',
    data: [
        {name: 'USA', x:78.09, y:2.05, z:307007000},
        {name: 'Canada', x:80.66, y:1.67, z:33739900}
```

```
        ]
    }, {
      name: 'Europe',
      data: [
        {name: 'Russia', x:68.6, y:1.54, z:141850000},
        {name: 'Germany', x:79.84, y:1.36, z:81902307},
        {name: 'Great Britain', x:80.05, y:2, z:61801570},
        {name: 'Denmark', x:78.6, y:1.84, z:5523095}
      ]
    }, {
      name: 'Middle East',
      data: [
        {name: 'Iraq', x:68.09, y:4.77, z:31090763},
        {name: 'Egypt', x:72.73, y:2.78, z:79716203},
        {name: 'Iran', x:72.49, y:1.7, z:73137148}
      ]
    }]
  });
```

By setting the chart's `type` parameter to `bubble` and providing data points containing life expectancy, fertility rate, and population of the country respectively, we plot the bubble chart showing the correlation between these values.

The preceding code produces the following bubble chart:

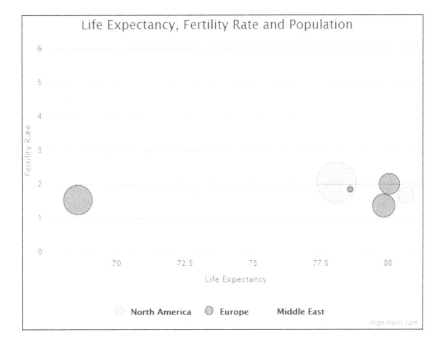

We formatted the tooltip using the `pointFormat` property to properly show the values, as shown in the following screenshot:

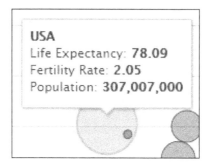

In bubble charts, *x* and *y* values behave the same as the 2D charts, whereas the third variable (in this case `Population`) affects the size of the bubble. The bubbles with a higher radius in the previous chart represent a higher population and vice versa.

Summary

In this chapter, you learned about area charts, stacking them, and plotting with percentage values to get a proportional overview of the plotted data. You also learned about sharing tooltips between multiple series so as to view the current point data with just a single hover. Then, we moved on to area-spline charts that are based on spline charts that have similar configuration options to those of area charts. Next, we began exploring the scatter chart and looked at yet another technique to modify tooltips with minimal programming needed. You also learned about using custom data marker symbols. In the last part, we used a bubble chart to plot 3D data.

In the next chapter, you will learn about pie, polar, and spider web charts and their combinations with other chart types, along with their various configuration options and how we can use them to maximize the readability of our raw data.

5
Pie, Polar, and Spider Web Charts

This chapter is devoted to pie, polar, and spider web charts. We will learn about these charts along with their construction and configuration options. We will:

- Plot basic pie charts
- Slice off pie charts
- Configure a pie chart for drilldown
- Create a semicircle donut
- Combine a donut chart with different chart types
- Create a polar chart
- Configure wind rose and spider web charts

At the end of this chapter, we will learn about spider web charts and how to tweak their configuration options to turn them into wind rose charts.

Introducing pie charts

Pie charts are a special kind of chart as they don't have x and y axes; rather, they are circular charts divided into slices where each slice represents a proportion of the actual data. They are most suitable for visualizing data that is meant to be shown proportionally or in percentages. The percentage of each category is usually shown next to the corresponding slice.

To gain more insight into a pie chart and its various configuration options that Highcharts provides, we are going to plot a pie chart representing the market share of desktop operating systems:

```javascript
(function() {
  $( '#chart_container' ).highcharts({
    chart: {
      type: 'pie'
    },
    title: {
      text: 'Desktop Operating Systems Marketshare'
    },
    subtitle: {
      text: 'StatCounter'
    },
    tooltip: {
      valueSuffix: '%'
    },
    series: [{
      name: 'Operating Systems',
      data: [
        ['Windows', 88.19],
        ['MacOSX', 9.22],
        ['Linux', 1.58],
        ['Others', 1.01]
      ]
    }]
  });
})();
```

Notice that we haven't defined the axes in the preceding code but rather gave data points in terms of an array. This array contains the name of the category as the first element and its quantity as the second one. The proportion of each category will be calculated by summing up all the values and then dividing individual values by this sum. Each slice in the circle will represent the proportion or percentage of its respective category.

The preceding code will produce the following pie chart:

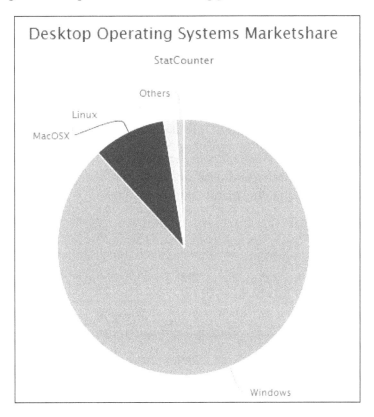

We have also configured the tooltip to append a % sign at the end of the category value when someone hovers over the chart:

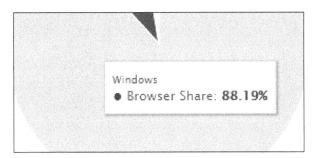

The tooltip now shows the percentage sign prefixed with the percentage number.

It's worth mentioning here that we don't need to provide percentages as data. We could also provide absolute numbers and then show their relative percentages in data labels and tooltips using the `pointFormat` property, as shown in the following code:

```
tooltip: {
  pointFormat: '{series.name}: <b>{point.percentage:.2f}%</b>'
},
dataLabels: {
  pointFormat: '{series.name}: <b>{point.percentage:.2f}%</b>'
},
```

This will ensure that the tooltip and data labels show the relative percentages of the data points instead of their actual numbers.

Having learned about basic pie chart construction, we will now learn about slicing it off in the next section.

Slicing off a pie chart

Slicing off a pie chart can be useful if we need to distinguish a particular category from the rest. The sliced-off category displays a little outwards from the main chart.

In the following example, we will take a look at how we can slice off a particular category in pie charts. So modify the code from the previous example to slice off the `MacOSX` category:

```
series: [{
  name: 'Operating Systems',
  data: [
    ['Windows', 88.19],
    {
      name: 'MacOSX',
      y: 9.22,
      sliced: true
    },
    ['Linux', 1.58],
    ['Others', 1.01]
  ]
}]
```

We replaced the array containing the category name and the value with an object in which we have explicitly defined these properties along with the `sliced` property. By enabling the `sliced` property, the category will be sliced off from the main chart.

The preceding snippet also shows the simplicity and flexibility of the Highcharts API. In most cases, where slicing is not required, we can define categories as an array containing the category name and its value. On the other hand, for more advanced modification, Highcharts provides us with an object, containing all the properties at our disposal.

A sliced-off chart will look like the following screenshot:

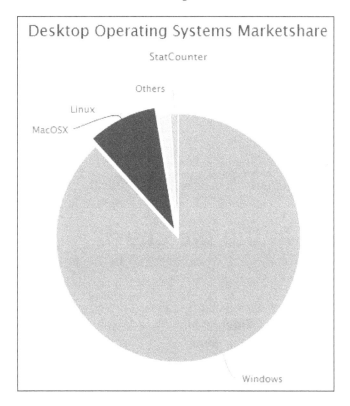

Enabling slicing by point selection

The point selection is turned off by default in a Highcharts configuration, but we can enable it to allow the slicing off of categories by selecting them. We can achieve this result by enabling the `sliced` and `selected` properties in the category while setting the `allowPointSelect` property to `true` in the `plotOptions` component:

```
plotOptions: {
  pie: {
    dataLabels: {
      enabled: true
    },
```

```
      allowPointSelect: true
    }
  },
  series: [{
    name: 'Operating Systems',
    data: [
      ['Windows', 88.19],
      {
        name: 'MacOSX',
        y: 9.22,
        sliced: true,
        selected: true
      },
      ['Linux', 1.58],
      ['Others', 1.01]
    ]
  }]
```

Now any category in the chart can be sliced off by selecting it.

Drilling down the pie chart

Just as we drilled down column charts, pie charts can also be drilled down to show
a particular category in more detail.

In the following code, taken from the previous example, we drill down the generic
Windows category to show a different version of Windows being used:

```
  series: [{
    name: 'Operating Systems',
    data: [
      {
        name: 'Windows',
        y: 88.19,
        drilldown: 'windows-versions'
      },
      ['MacOSX', 9.22],
      ['Linux', 1.58],
      ['Others', 1.01]
    ]
  }],
  drilldown: {
    series: [{
      name: 'Windows versions',
```

```
    id: 'windows-versions',
    data: [
      ['Win 7', 55.03],
      ['Win XP', 15.83],
      ['Win Vista', 3.59],
      ['Win 8', 7.56],
      ['Win 8.1', 6.18]
    ]
  }]
}
```

Be sure to include the `Highcharts-4.x.x/js/modules/drilldown.js` file before the `highcharts.js` file, as shown in the following code:

```
<script src="/js/highcharts.js"></script>
<script src="/js/modules/drilldown.js"></script>
```

As mentioned in *Chapter 2, Column and Bar Charts*, not including the `Highcharts-4.x.x/js/modules/drilldown.js` file will cause the drilldown feature not to work. This will not produce any errors, hence making debugging very difficult.

We have specified the `drilldown` property for the series we want to drilldown. The `drilldown` property is the ID of the drilldown series. Now, when you click on the `Windows` series in the chart, you will be taken to the drilled down pie chart.

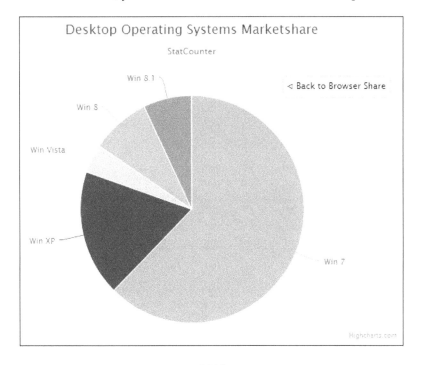

You can go back to the main chart by clicking on the **Back to Browser Share** button at the top-right corner of the chart.

Modifying the back button

By default, the back button will display text in the **Back to {Parent Series}** format. You can modify it by accessing the `drillUpText` property in the `lang` component:

```
lang: {
  drillUpText: 'Back to main chart'
}
```

The `lang` component is where we define the language settings and the text for different scenarios. We will look at the `lang` component in more detail in *Chapter 7, Theming with Highcharts*, although you can always refer to the official documentation at `http://api.highcharts.com/highcharts#lang`.

The position and appearance of the button can also be customized by modifying various properties in the `drilldown.drillUpButton` component:

```
drillUpButton: {
  position: {
    x: 10,
    y: -20,
    align: 'left',
    verticalAlign: 'bottom'
  },
  theme: {
    fill: '#f28149',
    stroke: '#f27130',
    r: 5,
    style: {
      color: '#ffffff'
    },
    states: {
      hover: {
        fill: '#f26118',
        stroke: '#f26118'
      }
    }
  }
}
```

The theme supports various SVG properties such as `fill`, `stroke`, `stroke-width`, and `r` (for radius). The button state for a mouse hover is defined inside the `states` element.

The following screenshot shows the customized button:

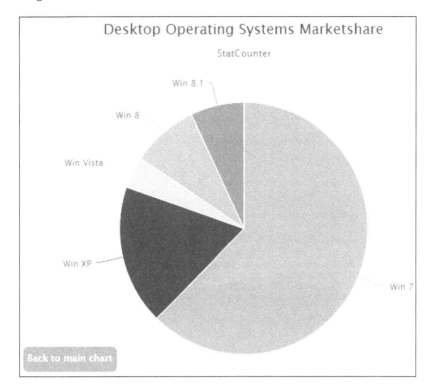

Creating a 3D pie chart

Pie chart is also supported by the Highcharts 3D module. In the following code, we will take data from the previous example. The data shows the breakdown of the market share of the Windows operating system.

The `plotOptions` component and the `chart.options3d` object are as follows:

```
chart: {
  type: 'pie',
  options3d: {
    enabled: true,
    alpha: 60,
    beta: 0
  }
},
```

```
plotOptions: {
  pie: {
    dataLabels: {
      enabled: true
    },
    allowPointSelect: true,
    depth: 50
  }
}
```

This will produce the following 3D pie chart:

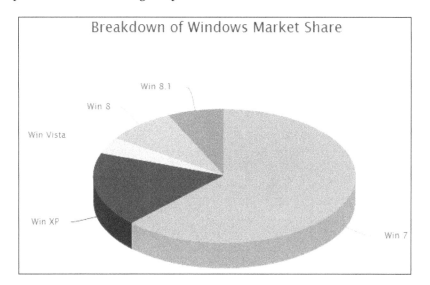

Creating pie charts with multiple series

We can also choose to show two different pie charts in a single chart by adding two series. These two charts will appear side by side in a single container, although we can also modify their positions within the container to meet our needs. These types of charts are great for comparing the data of different series.

Consider the very first example of this chapter where we created a simple pie chart to show the market share of popular desktop operating systems. We will use the same series for the first pie chart and introduce a second series to show the market share of mobile operating systems:

```
series: [{
  name: 'Desktop OS Marketshare',
```

```
      center: ['25%', '50%'],
      size: '50%',
      data: [
        ['Windows', 88.19],
        ['MacOSX', 9.22],
        ['Linux', 1.58],
        ['Others', 1.01]
      ]
    }, {
      name: 'Mobile OS Marketshare',
      center: ['75%', '50%'],
      size: '50%',
      data: [
        ['Android', 77.83],
        ['iOS', 17.8],
        ['Microsoft', 2.94],
        ['RIM', 0.72],
        ['Symbian', 0.71]
      ]
    }]
```

We have centered the first pie chart at 25 percent along the horizontal and the second at 75 percent. The vertical alignment for both the pie charts is the same, that is, 50 percent along the vertical with respect to the container. Notice that the size of the container has been increased to 1000 px x 600 px to accommodate the two pie charts.

The following is a screenshot of a multi-pie chart:

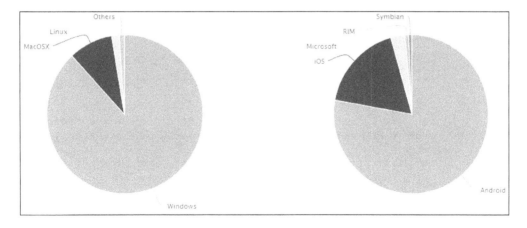

So far in this chapter, we have learned about pie charts and their configuration options. We learned about creating simple pie charts, configuring them for drilldown, and even created two side-by-side pie charts in a single chart. In the following section, we will begin learning about donut charts.

Creating a donut chart

In a previous example, we created a pie chart with a drilldown feature; that is, when a user clicks on the parent category, he is taken to another chart showing the breakdown of that parent category in more detail. If we want to show this detailed breakdown of data right in the main chart, we will need to use a donut chart. This is where donut charts are most useful, as they display the breakdown of the parent category without the need for the drilldown feature.

Consider the example of the top three car manufacturers (by sales) in the United States. Their sales for December 2013 to December 2014 for their best-seller models are as follows:

- 154,491 Ford cars
- 90,080 Honda cars
- 93,460 Chevy cars

We can visualize this data with the help of a pie chart using the following code:

```
(function() {
  $( '#chart_container' ).highcharts({
    chart: {
      type: 'pie'
    },
    title: {
      text: 'Car Sales for December 2013 - 2014'
    },
    subtitle: {
      text: 'Source: <a href="http://www.businessinsider.com/best-
selling-cars-in-december-2013-2014-1?op=1">Business Insider</a>',
      useHTML: true
    },
    plotOptions: {
      pie: {
        dataLabels: {
          enabled: false
        },
```

```
        borderColor: 'rgba(255, 255, 255, 0.2)'
      }
    },
    series: [{
      name: 'Car Manufacturers',
      innerSize: '60%',
      dataLabels: {
        enabled: true,
        distance: -40,
        color: '#ffffff'
      },
      data: [
        {name: 'Chevy', y: 93460, color: 'rgba(135, 43, 36, 1)'},
        {name: 'Ford', y: 154491, color: 'rgba(38, 85, 182, 1)'},
        {name: 'Honda', y: 90080, color: 'rgba(104, 135, 36, 1)'}
      ]
    }]
  });
})();
```

Please note that we have used a pie chart as our chart type since donuts are also pie charts, but with a different appearance.

This will create a simple pie chart as follows:

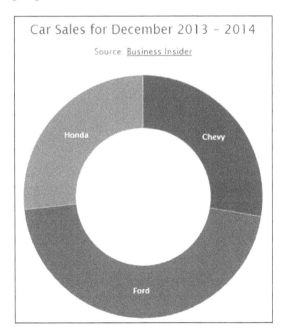

Notice the use of the `innerSize` property that created an empty space in the middle of the chart when we set it to `60%`. We will fit the series containing detailed data of sales inside this empty space by utilizing its `size` property. Insert the following series inside the series array:

```
{
  name: 'Car Models',
  size: '54%',
  data: [
    {name: 'Malibu', y: 15493, color: 'rgba(135, 43, 36, 0.9)'},
    {name: 'Equinox', y: 17212, color: 'rgba(135, 43, 36, 0.9)'},
    {name: 'Cruze', y: 18162, color: 'rgba(135, 43, 36, 0.9)'},
    {name: 'Silverado', y: 42593, color: 'rgba(135, 43, 36, 0.9)'},
    {name: 'Focus', y: 15569, color: 'rgba(38, 85, 182, 0.9)'},
    {name: 'Explorer', y: 15660, color: 'rgba(38, 85, 182, 0.9)'},
    {name: 'Escape', y: 24262, color: 'rgba(38, 85, 182, 0.9)'},
    {name: 'Fusion', y: 24408, color: 'rgba(38, 85, 182, 0.9)'},
    {name: 'F-Series', y: 74592, color: 'rgba(38, 85, 182, 0.9)'},
    {name: 'CR-V', y: 28759, color: 'rgba(104, 135, 36, 0.9)'},
    {name: 'Civic', y: 29000, color: 'rgba(104, 135, 36, 0.9)'},
    {name: 'Accord', y: 32321, color: 'rgba(104, 135, 36, 0.9)'}
  ]
}
```

Note that we have given car manufacturers and their respective models the same color to distinguish them from other manufacturers. The only difference in the colors of car manufacturers and their car models is that we have set the `alpha` value of the car models to `0.9`. This is to create a visual relationship between the car models and their manufacturers.

Since we have given the second series a size of 54%, it will shrink to fit inside the empty space, as shown in the following chart. The categories in the inner chart will align with their respective parent categories in the outer chart since their values total to the value of their respective parent category.

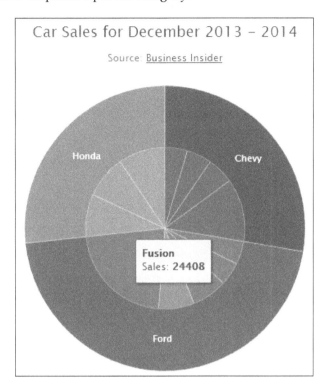

Configuring a semicircle donut

Highcharts also offers a semicircle donut chart, a variation of the pie chart. Converting a pie chart into a semicircle donut is easy as it requires just setting the startAngle and endAngle properties.

Take the code from the previous example and remove the second series for the sake of simplicity. You will be left with a series containing car manufacturers, and we will be converting it into a semicircle donut chart using the following code:

```
plotOptions: {
  pie: {
    startAngle: -90,
    endAngle: 90
  }
}
```

The chart will now start at 90° to the left and end at 90° to the right.

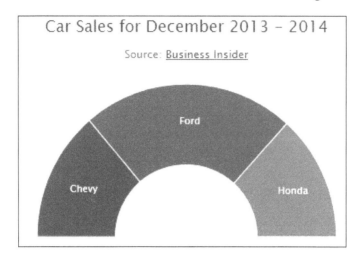

You can play quite a lot with the startAngle and endAngle properties. The following is a screenshot of a quarter-circle chart that is produced by setting startAngle to -180° and endAngle to 90°:

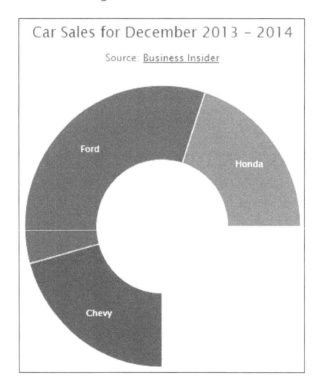

Setting the `innerSize` property of the series to `20%` produces the following result:

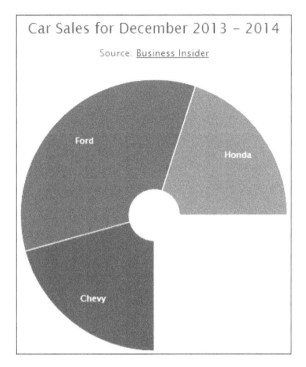

Combining pie charts with line and column charts

In *Chapter 3*, *Line and Spline Charts*, we combined the line and the column chart. In the following example, we will take a look at how to combine a pie chart with a column and line chart to present data via three different chart types for greater data visualization.

Consider the example of fuel consumption by the United States, China, and the European Union in the year 2012 by fuel type. First, the data for the first two countries will be plotted by the column graph whereas the data for the EU will be visualized by the line chart. We will then plot the total fuel consumption by type using a pie chart that will appear along with the main chart.

The following is the code for the line and column chart combination:

```
(function() {
  $( '#chart_container' ).highcharts({
    title: {
      text: 'Fuel Consumption by Type for the Year 2012'
    },
    subtitle: {
      text: 'Source: <a href="http://bp.com">BP</a>',
      useHTML: true
    },
    xAxis: {
      categories: ['Oil', 'Natural Gas', 'Coal',
        'Nuclear Energy', 'Hydroelectricity', 'Renewable']
    },
    yAxis: {
      title: {
        text: 'Million Metric Tons of Oil Equivalent'
      }
    },
    series: [{
      name: 'U.S.',
      type: 'column',
      data: [819.9, 654, 437.4, 183.2, 63.2, 50.7]
    }, {
      name: 'China',
      type: 'column',
      data: [483.7, 129.5, 1873.3, 22, 194.8, 31.9]
    }, {
      name: 'EU',
      type: 'line',
      data: [618.8, 399.7, 293.4, 199.9, 76.1, 97.7]
    }]
  });
})();
```

Instead of giving a chart type directly to the chart itself, we set the series type on individual series. The first two series for the United States and China are set as columns and the series for the EU is of the line type. Since both column and line charts require categories on the *x* axis, we defined our categories array, that is, the fuel types in the xAxis component.

The following is the combination produced by the preceding code:

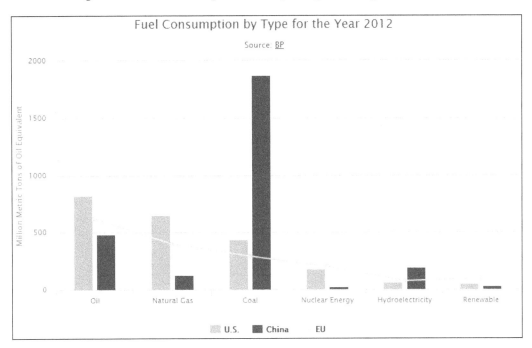

To introduce a pie chart that shows the total fuel consumption by type, we need another series of type pie. Refer to the following code:

```
{
  name: 'Total',
  type: 'pie',
  data: [
    {name: 'Oil', y: 1922.4},
    {name: 'Nuclear Energy', y: 405.1},
    {name: 'Coal', y: 2604.1},
    {name: 'Hydroelectricity', y: 334.1},
    {name: 'Natural Gas', y: 1183.2},
    {name: 'Renewable', y: 180.3}
  ],
  size: '80%',
  center: ['80%', '40%']
}
```

We also need to configure the data labels to show inside pie slices. We can do it by accessing the dataLabels object inside the Total series or by modifying the plotOptions.pie.dataLabels object:

```
plotOptions: {
  pie: {
    dataLabels: {
      distance: -45,
      color: '#ffffff'
    }
  }
}
```

This will bring the pie chart in the existing combination, as follows:

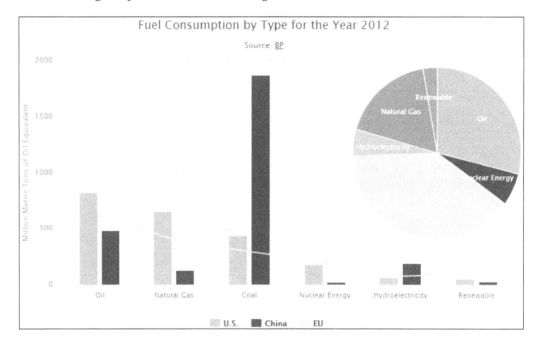

Introducing a polar chart

A polar chart is a circular chart in which data points are plotted at a distance and angle from the center of the circle. The categories for the x axis are located along the circumference of the circle whereas the labels for the y axis are located inside the circle at a certain distance from the center. A polar chart can plot one or more series, and it is best used to compare the data between different series.

Consider the data from the previous example that shows the fuel consumption by the EU. We can plot this data using a polar chart since the data is based on the type of fuel (categories).

The following code draws the polar chart for the mentioned data:

```
(function() {
  $( '#chart_container' ).highcharts({
    chart: {
      polar: true
    },
    title: {
      text: 'Fuel Consumption by Type for the Year 2012'
    },
    subtitle: {
      text: 'Source: <a href="http://bp.com">BP</a>',
      useHTML: true
    },
    pane: {
      startAngle: 0,
      endAngle: 360
    },
    xAxis: {
      categories: ['Oil', 'Natural Gas', 'Coal',
        'Nuclear Energy', 'Hydroelectricity', 'Renewable']
    },
    yAxis: {
      title: {
        text: 'MMT'
      }
    },
    series: [{
      name: 'EU',
      type: 'column',
      data: [618.8, 399.7, 293.4, 199.9, 76.1, 97.7]
    }]
  });
})();
```

In order for this code to work, include the `Highcharts-4.x.x/js/highcharts-more.js` file after the `highcharts.js` file on the page.

By setting the `polar` property on `chart` to `true`, we enabled the polar chart functionality. Individual series can then be given their own type as we have given the `column` type to the EU series.

In the `pane` component, we have set two properties: `startAngle` and `endAngle`. The default values are `0` and `360` respectively, but you can give your custom values depending on the type of data you are plotting.

The following is the screenshot of the chart produced by the preceding code:

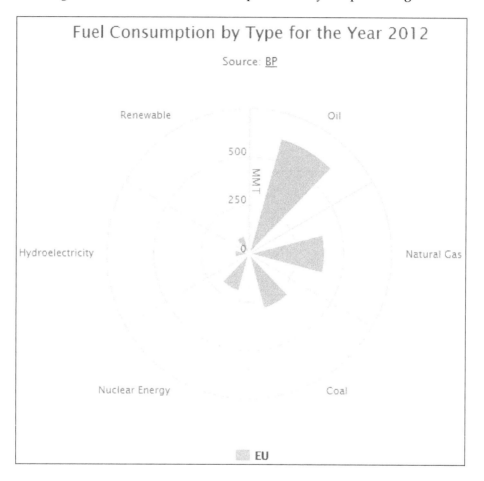

Polar charts with different series types

Each series in a polar chart can be given its individual series type. This enables us to combine different series types in a single polar chart.

Consider the following two series for the United States and China respectively, showing their fuel consumption by fuel type. The types are `line` and `area` respectively:

```
{
  name: 'U.S.',
  type: 'line',
  data: [819.9, 654, 437.4, 183.2, 63.2, 50.7]
}, {
  name: 'China',
  type: 'area',
  data: [483.7, 129.5, 1873.3, 22, 194.8, 31.9]
}
```

The chart now has three series with different series types. The polar chart produced after you introduce the preceding two series will be as follows:

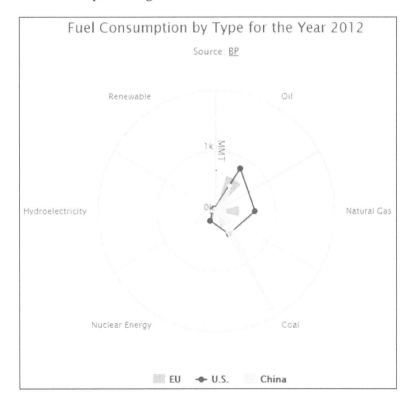

Converting other chart types to the polar chart

Various chart types, including column, bar, line, spline, and area charts, can be converted into a polar chart by simply including `Highcharts-4.x.x/js/highcharts-more.js` in the page and then setting the `polar` property on the chart to `true`.

Consider the first example in the *Introducing column charts* section from *Chapter 2, Column and Bar Charts*, in which we visualized the Olympics medal table using a column chart. The inclusion of `highcharts-more.js` to the page and the following modification will convert it into a polar chart:

```
$( '#medal_table' ).highcharts({
  chart: {
    polar: true
  },
  title: {
    text: 'Olympics 2012 Medal Table'
  },
  xAxis: {
    title: {
      text: 'Countries'
    },
    categories: ['United States', 'China',
      'Russian Federation', 'Great Britain', 'South Korea']
  },
  series: [{
    name: 'Medals',
    data: [104, 88, 82, 65, 28],
    type: 'column'
  }]
});
```

The result is as follows:

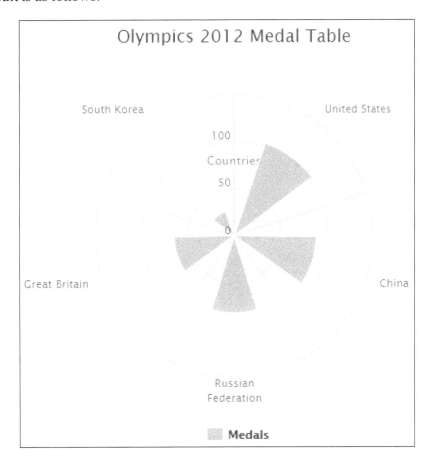

Introducing the spider web chart

A spider web chart is just like a polar chart but, instead of being a circle, it's polygonal in shape. In the following example, we will take the same data we used in the previous example but, this time, we'll plot it with a spider web chart:

```
(function() {
  $( '#medal_table' ).highcharts({
    chart: {
      polar: true
```

```
        },
        title: {
          text: 'Olympics 2012 Medal Table'
        },
        xAxis: {
          title: {
            text: 'Countries'
          },
          categories: ['United States', 'China',
            'Russian Federation', 'Great Britain', 'South Korea'],
          lineWidth: 0,
          tickmarkPlacement: 'on'
        },
        yAxis: {
          gridLineInterpolation: 'polygon'
        },
        series: [{
          name: 'Medals',
          data: [104, 88, 82, 65, 28],
          type: 'column'
        }]
      });
    })();
```

Hence, the code is the same as that of a polar chart, except for some properties in the axes. These include `lineWidth`, `gridLineInterpolation`, and `tickmarkPlacement`.

Setting the `lineWidth` property to `0` on the `xAxis` component removes the outer circle border that would otherwise appear enclosing the polygonal. By default, the value of `gridLineInterpolation` is `circle` that produces a circular polar chart. We changed it to `polygon` to produce a polygonal spider web chart.

The following is a spider web chart produced as a result of this modification:

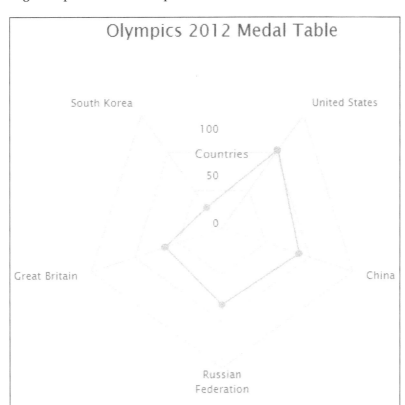

Creating a wind rose chart

A wind rose chart is created by enabling column stacking option in a series. Though it's not a very common type of chart, it's worth looking at, given that it's based on polar charts.

Consider the following modified code of an example from *Chapter 2, Column and Bar Charts*, that shows the breakdown of medals earned by leading countries in Olympics 2012. Notice the effect of enabling the column stacking option:

```
(function() {
  $( '#medal_table' ).highcharts({
    chart: {
      type: 'column',
```

```
      polar: true
    },
    title: {
      text: 'Olympics 2012 Medal Table'
    },
    xAxis: {
      title: {
        text: 'Countries'
      },
      categories: ['United States', 'China',
        'Russian Federation', 'Great Britain', 'South Korea']
    },
    yAxis: {
      title: {
        text: 'Medals',
        y: -45
      }
    },
    plotOptions: {
      column: {
        stacking: 'normal'
      }
    },
    series: [{
      name: 'Gold',
      data: [46, 38, 24, 29, 13]
    }, {
      name: 'Silver',
      data: [29, 27, 26, 17, 8]
    }, {
      name: 'Bronze',
      data: [29, 23, 32, 19, 7]
    }]
  });
}) ();
```

This will draw the following wind rose chart:

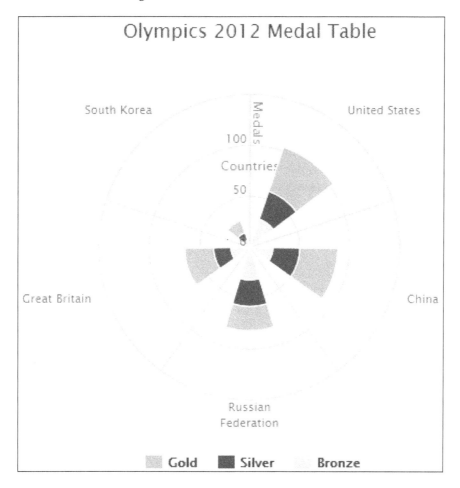

This shows how easy it is to convert an existing column chart that has stacking enabled to a wind rose chart with appealing visuals.

Summary

Here we end our journey exploring pie and polar charts and their variants. We learned to plot basic pie charts, sliced them off, and configured them for the drilldown feature. We used the 3D module to create a 3D pie chart and then created a single chart with two pie series side by side. We also learned to convert a pie chart into a donut chart and then combined pie charts with other different types of charts. Then we started creating polar charts; by tweaking their configuration options, we created several other chart types such as wind rose and spider web.

We have almost completed exploring major chart types that Highcharts provides. In the next chapter, we will look at some other chart types, including gauges, pyramid charts, funnel charts, and heat maps.

6
Other Chart Types

In this chapter, we will learn about chart types that are different from the commonly used ones and use different configuration options. These include angular gauge, solid gauge, VU meter, waterfall chart, pyramid chart, funnel chart, and finally, a heat map. To be specific, we will cover the following topics:

- Creating and configuring an angular gauge
- Plot a solid gauge chart
- Create a VU meter
- Plotting and funneling pyramid charts
- Drawing a heat map—a new chart type introduced in Highcharts 4

 In order to follow the upcoming examples in this chapter, it's necessary to include the `highcharts-4.x.x/js/highcharts-more.js` file in your page after the `highcharts.js` file to add support for more chart types.

Creating an angular gauge chart

Angular gauge charts are also known as speedometers and dials. They are great to use on dashboards, especially when the plotted data is being fetched in real time. These charts don't contain the x axis, but instead, they contain only one value axis, that is, the y axis. Anything provided for the x axis will not be drawn on the chart.

In the following example, we will plot a simple angular gauge chart to take a look at the configuration options it offers:

```
$( '#chart_container' ).highcharts({
  chart: {
    type: 'gauge'
  },
```

```
    title: {
      text: 'Speedometer'
    },
    pane: {
      startAngle: -150,
      endAngle: 150
    },
    yAxis: {
      title: {
        text: 'km/h'
      },
      min: 0,
      max: 200
    },
    series: [{
      name: 'Speed',
      data: [120]
    }]
});
```

Nothing much is going on here as we declared the chart type to be gauge. Then, for the pane component, we defined its start and end angles at `-150` and `150`, respectively. This will create a simple gauge chart as follows:

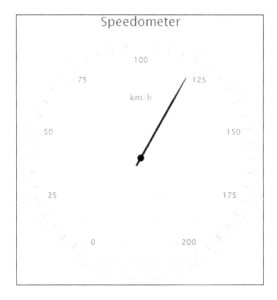

You can find more about the pane component by visiting the official documentation at http://api.highcharts.com/highcharts#pane.

An angular gauge with dual axes

In the previous example, we created an angular gauge with a single axis, but we can also create an angular gauge with multiple axes. The yAxis component accepts an array to define multiple axes. Each axis can have its own configuration options and styling, as shown in the following code:

```
yAxis: [{
  min: 0,
  max: 200,
  offset: -40,
  labels: {
    style: {
      color: '#2085e6'
    }
  },
  lineColor: '#2085e6',
  lineWidth: 3,
  tickColor: '#2085e6',
  tickWidth: 3,
  minorTickColor: '#2085e6',
  minorTickWidth: 1
}, {
  min: 0,
  max: 124,
  tickPosition: 'outside',
  minorTickPosition: 'outside',
  offset: -30,
  labels: {
    style: {
      color: '#e63820'
    },
    distance: 20
  },
  lineColor: '#e63820',
  lineWidth: 3,
  tickColor: '#e63820',
  tickWidth: 3,
  minorTickColor: '#e63820',
  minorTickWidth: 1
}]
```

The preceding code will give the following result:

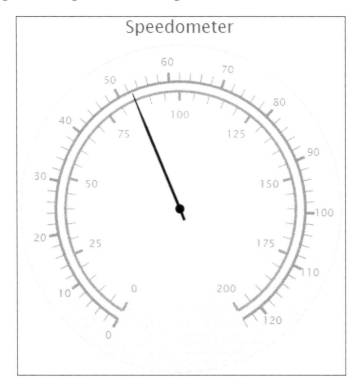

When introducing dual axes, it's important to calculate the unit difference in both axes, hence defining the max and min values accordingly. For instance, in the preceding example that shows the speed in kmph and mph, we know that 1 km is equal to 0.621 miles; hence, for the max value of 200 km on one axis, the corresponding max value on the other axis is set to be 124 miles.

In addition to the modified yAxis, the chart.alignTicks property has also been set to false to prevent Highcharts from aligning the ticks of both the axes, hence resulting in the max value for one of the axes being ignored.

Styling the angular gauge

As with all the charts offered by Highcharts, the angular gauge chart can be customized heavily to incorporate the branding of an application or a website. We have taken a look at how to modify various styling options for each axis in the previous example. We will take it a bit further in the following example to give the speedometer a more fancy look.

We will begin by customizing the look of the axes. To do so, we will modify various properties, including `labels`, `lineColor`, `lineWidth`, and `tickColor`. The following code will modify both the axes:

```
yAxis: [{
  min: 0,
  max: 220,
  offset: -110,
  labels: {
    style: {
      color: '#fff'
    }
  },
  lineColor: '#e63820',
  lineWidth: 0,
  tickColor: '#e63820',
  tickWidth: 3,
  tickLength: 12,
  minorTickColor: '#e63820',
  minorTickWidth: 3,
  minorTickLength: 6,
  minorTickInterval: 10
}, {
  min: 0,
  max: 140,
  offset: -40,
  labels: {
    style: {
      'font-size': '21px',
      'font-family': 'arial, sans-serif',
      color: '#ffffff'
    },
    distance: -45
  },
  lineColor: '#e63820',
  lineWidth: 0,
  tickLength: 20,
  tickColor: '#e63820',
  tickWidth: 4,
  minorTickInterval: 2,
  minorTickColor: '#e63820',
  minorTickWidth: 4,
  minorTickLength: 10
}]
```

In this code, we gave `min` and `max` values to each axis that are relative to each other. Then we defined the offset so that one axis shows inside the other in the chart. For both the axes, we modified the properties relating to line, tick, and minor ticks, including their color, width, and length.

Now for the chart background, we might want to set a background image instead of using just a plain color or a default gradient. For this, we need to modify the pane and chart components:

```
chart: {
  type: 'gauge',
  plotBackgroundImage: 'img/blackorchid.png',
  alignTicks: false
},
pane: {
  startAngle: -150,
  endAngle: 150,
  background: [{
    backgroundColor: 'none',
    borderColor: 'none'
  }]
}
```

By setting the `backgroundColor` and `borderColor` properties in `pane` to `transparent`, we made sure that the background image we set for the chart is displayed behind the pane too.

Then for the final part, we need to customize the dial needle that points to the values on the axes. This can be accessed in `plotOptions.gauge.gauge`, as shown in the following code:

```
plotOptions: {
  gauge: {
    dial: {
      radius: '80%',
      backgroundColor: '#fff',
      baseWidth: 6,
      rearLength: '10%'
    }
  }
}
```

The full code can be found in the code examples accompanying this book.

The chart produced as a result of all of this customization will look like the following screenshot:

Creating a VU meter

A VU meter is the same as an angular gauge but, instead of having a full circle-like shape, it's more like an arc. All the configuration options that we learned for the angular gauge chart apply to the VU meter as well.

In the following example, we will create a simple VU meter to plot the global emission of CO2 in the year 2012:

```
$( '#chart_container' ).highcharts({
  chart: {
    type: 'gauge',
    plotBackgroundColor: 'none'
  },
  title: {
    text: 'Global CO<sub>2</sub> Emission in 2012 (in billion metric
tons)',
    useHTML: true
  },
  pane: {
    startAngle: -45,
    endAngle: 45,
```

```
      background: {
        backgroundColor: 'none',
        borderColor: 'none'
      },
      size: 400,
      center: ['50%', '60%']
    },
    tooltip: {
      enabled: false
    },
    plotOptions: {
      gauge: {
        dial: {
          radius: '95%'
        }
      }
    },
    yAxis: {
      min: 0,
      max: 16,
      tickInterval: 2,
      tickPosition: 'outside',
      minorTickInterval: 0,
      labels: {
        distance: 20
      },
      plotBands: [{
        from: 0,
        to: 4,
        color: '#3dbf24'
      }, {
        from: 4,
        to: 12,
        color: '#dc841c'
      }, {
        from: 12,
        to: 16,
        color: '#dc401c'
      }]
    },
    series: [{
      data: [12]
    }]
  });
```

We turned off the default circle background of the angular gauge by setting `pane.background.backgroundColor` to `none`. This will remove the default gray gradient that appears behind the pane in a circular shape. The `startAngle` and `endAngle` properties have been set to `-45` and `45` respectively to create an arc-like shape for the pane. The `plotBands` array in the `yAxis` component enhances visualization by adding color bands for various value ranges.

The following is a screenshot of the VU meter produced as a result of the preceding code:

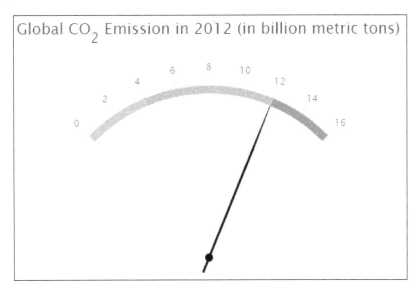

Creating a solid gauge

Solid gauges were introduced in Highcharts 4 and they are similar to angular gauges, except that they use solid colors to display the value. This color responds to the value on the y axis, and we can define the colors that correspond to different value ranges in `yAxis.stops` in an array.

Consider the following example in which we will configure a solid gauge:

```
$( '#chart_container' ).highcharts({
  chart: {
    type: 'solidgauge'
  },
  title: {
    text: 'Speedometer'
  },
```

```
pane: {
  startAngle: -90,    endAngle: 90,
  background: {
    backgroundColor: 'none',
    borderColor: '#aaa',
    innerRadius: '100%',
    outerRadius: '60%',
    shape: 'arc'
  }
},
plotOptions: {
  solidgauge: {
    dataLabels: {
            y: -40,
            borderWidth: 0,
            useHTML: true
        }
  }
},
tooltip: {
  enabled: false
},
yAxis: {
  title: {
    text: 'km/h',
    align: 'low',
    x: -15
  },
  stops: [
    [0.1, '#50bf39'],
    [0.4, '#9ebf39'],
    [0.7, '#bf9e39'],
    [0.9, '#bf3939']
  ],
  min: 0,
  max: 200,
  lineWidth: 0,
  tickWidth: 0,
  minorTickWidth: 0,
  labels: {
    enabled: false
  }
},
```

```
    series: [{
      name: 'Speed',
      data: [120]
    }]
  });
```

Notice the pane component where we have set `startAngle` and `endAngle` to `90` and `-90` respectively. This will give the gauge chart its turned-over U-shape. The next two properties `innerRadius` and `outerRadius` define the `arc` shape of the gauge.

The `stops` property takes an array for color values that corresponds to the value ranges on the *y* axis. We have defined four stops for four value ranges. Value ranges can be defined by a number from 0 to 1 that represents the percent value across the pane.

The following is a screenshot of the solid gauge produced:

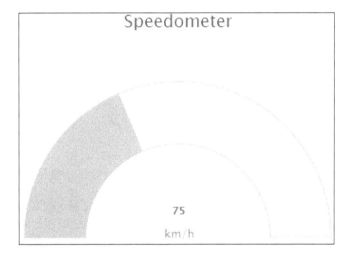

In this screenshot, the gauge shows the color green (`#9ebf39`) since the data we have plotted (75 kmph) falls within the range of the second stop.

In the next section, we will create a waterfall chart that is used to show data with cumulative values.

Plotting a waterfall chart

A waterfall chart displays the cumulative effect of the values. Each data point is accumulated on top of the previous data point or subtracted from the previous data point if the value is negative. This creates a flying bricks appearance due to the suspension of columns in midair.

Waterfall charts are most suitable in finance where one needs to visualize the cumulative effect of several positive and negative values.

In the following example, we will plot the budget breakdown of the London 2012 Olympics by the expense area:

```
$( '#chart_container' ).highcharts({
    chart: {
        type: 'waterfall'
    },
    title: {
        text: 'Budget of London 2012 Olympics'
    },
    xAxis: {
        type: 'category'
    },
    yAxis: {
        title: {
            text: 'US million dollars'
        }
    },
    tooltip: {
        valueSuffix: ' Million USD'
    },
    series: [{
        name: 'Budget',
        data: [
            {name: 'Venues', y: 4607},
            {name: 'Olympic Village', y: 1919},
            {name: 'CT operations', y: 1776},
            {name: 'Other projects', y: 1421},
            {name: 'Transport projects', y: 1392},
            {name: 'Anticipated final costs', y: 1311},
            {name: 'Legacy projects', y: 1298},
            {name: 'Olympic parkland', y: 1204},
            {name: 'Police', y: 943},
            {name: 'Venue security', y: 869},
            {name: 'Government bodies', y: 696},
```

```
                    {name: 'Contingency fund', y: 157},
                    {name: 'Ceremonies', y: 126}
                ]
            }]
    });
```

The data points are given in the form of an array containing the name and the value.

To show the cumulative budget, we can add another data point with the `isSum` property set to `true`:

```
{name: 'Total Budget', isSum: true}
```

This will produce a chart with a waterfall-like appearance, hence called a waterfall chart:

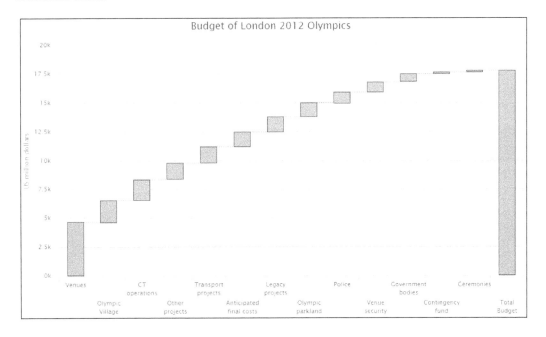

If you need to show the cumulative value in the middle of the series, you can do so by adding another data point and setting the `isIntermediateSum` property to `true`.

Plotting a pyramid chart

A pyramid chart is triangular in shape and divided into sections, with each data point representing a section. Because of the triangular shape, these sections are not equal in width, and hence the width doesn't necessarily represent the value of each data point. They are useful to show data that needs to be shown in a particular hierarchy.

 To plot pyramid and funnel charts, the `highcharts-4.x.x/js/modules/funnel.js` script is required.

We will take the data from the previous example to plot a pyramid chart of the London 2012 Olympics budget breakdown:

```
$( '#chart_container' ).highcharts({
    chart: {
        type: 'pyramid',
        marginLeft: -10
    },
    title: {
        text: 'Budget of London 2012 Olympics'
    },
    series: [{
        name: 'Budget',
        data: [
            ['Venues', 4607],
            ['Olympic Village', 1919],
            ['CT operations', 1776],
            ['Other projects', 1421],
            ['Transport projects', 1392],
            ['Anticipated final costs', 1311],
            ['Legacy projects', 1298],
            ['Olympic parkland', 1204],
            ['Police', 943],
            ['Venue security', 869],
            ['Government bodies', 696],
            ['Contingency fund', 157],
            ['Ceremonies', 126]
        ]
    }]
});
```

The following screenshot shows the resultant pyramid chart:

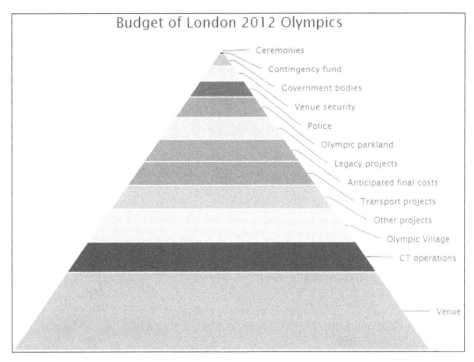

Drawing a funnel chart

The funnel chart is usually used to represent different stages of a sales process. Being shaped like a funnel, it's divided into different sections with each section representing a process stage. The top section represents the initial stage with most number of clients, while the bottom section is the final stage. Sections become narrower as we go down to the next stage, representing a drop in the number of clients, hence forming the shape of a funnel.

In the following example, we will take a look at how we can create a simple funnel chart:

```
$( '#chart_container' ).highcharts({
    chart: {
        type: 'funnel',
        marginLeft: -10
    },
    title: {
```

```
                    text: 'Representing a Typical Sales Project'
            },
            plotOptions: {
                    series: {
                            neckWidth: '25%',
                            neckHeight: '35%'
                    }
            },
            series: [{
                    name: 'Budget',
                    data: [
                            ['Website visits', 56147],
                            ['User subscriptions', 21045],
                            ['Quote requests', 10423],
                            ['Invoiced', 8750],
                            ['Final sales', 8459]
                    ]
            }]
    });
```

The neckWidth and neckHeight properties in the plotOptions.series determine the width and height of the funnel's neck respectively, as shown in the following screenshot:

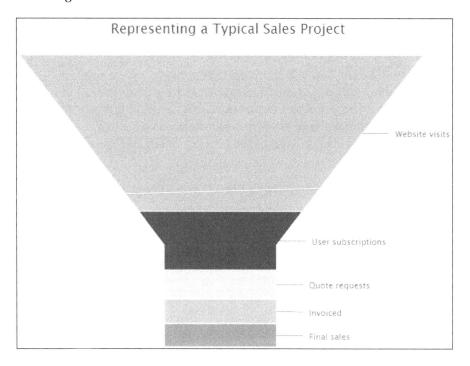

Hence funnel charts are useful to gain insights into the sales process and help determine the areas that need to be focused on more in order to increase sales.

Creating a heat map

Heat maps were added in Highcharts in Version 4. A heat map displays data in a graphical format using colors and color ranges. Each value is contained in a matrix and is assigned a mid-tone color among extreme colors based on its value. This creates a visual representation of values in the map.

The data points are given in the form of an array that contains three elements. The first two elements are zero-index-based position coordinates in the matrix, and the third element is the actual value of the data point.

 Be sure to include the `highcharts-4.x.x/js/modules/heatmap.js` file before you continue with the example.

In the following example, we will plot the monthly climate data for Toronto with the help of a heat map by utilizing its various configuration options:

```
$( '#chart_container' ).highcharts({
    chart: {
        type: 'heatmap'
    },
    title: {
        text: 'Monthy Temperature Statistics - Toronto'
    },
    subtitle: {
        text: 'Source: <a href="http://theweathernetwork.com"
target="_blank">The Weather Network</a>',
        useHTML: true
    },
    xAxis: {
        categories: ['Jan', 'Feb', 'Mar', 'Apr', 'May', 'Jun', 'Jul',
'Aug', 'Sep', 'Oct', 'Nov', 'Dec']
    },
    yAxis: {
        categories: ['Average high', 'Average low', 'Average'],
        title: null
    },
```

```
    series: [{
        name: 'Temperature',
        data: [[0, 0, -1.1], [1, 0, -0.2], [2, 0, 4.6], [3, 0, 11.3],
    [4, 0, 18.5], [5, 0, 23.5], [6, 0, 26.4], [7, 0, 25.3], [8, 0, 20.7],
    [9, 0, 13.8], [10, 0, 7.4], [11, 0, 1.8],
                [0, 1, -7.3], [1, 1, -6.3], [2, 1, -2], [3, 1, 3.8], [4,
    1, 9.9], [5, 1, 14.8], [6, 1, 17.9], [7, 1, 17.3], [8, 1, 13.2], [9,
    1, 7.3], [10, 1, 2.2], [11, 1, -3.7],
                [0, 2, -4.2], [1, 2, -3.2], [2, 2, 1.3], [3, 2, 7.6], [4,
    2, 14.2], [5, 2, 19.2], [6, 2, 22.2], [7, 2, 21.3], [8, 2, 17], [9, 2,
    10.6], [10, 2, 4.8], [11, 2, -0.9]]
    }]
});
```

Both the axes in the preceding code have categories to represent the month and temperature type. This will produce a fairly simple heat map with all the values represented by a single default color:

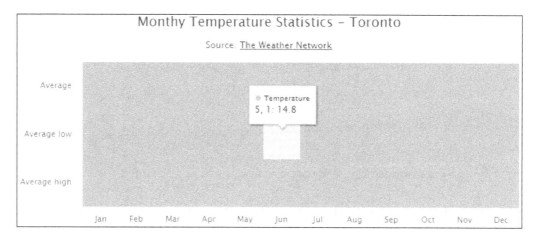

We will now bring in the color axis and format it to align its legend to the right of the chart:

```
colorAxis: {
    minColor: '#499eee',
    maxColor: '#f39a6f'
},
legend: {
    align: 'right',
```

```
        layout: 'vertical',
        symbolHeight: 235,
        y: -22
}
```

We have defined #499eee and #f39a6f as the minimum and maximum color values respectively in the colorAxis component. This will give the heat map its well-known appearance, as shown in the following screenshot:

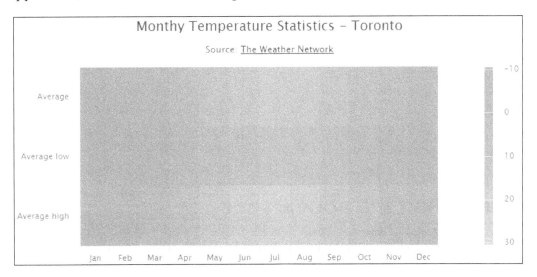

As you hover over data points in the chart, a marker will indicate the value range and its color in the legend. This marker can also be customized via the colorAxis.marker property, as shown in the following code:

```
colorAxis: {
    minColor: '#499eee',
    maxColor: '#f39a6f',
    marker: {
        animation: {
            duration: 100
        },
        color: 'red',
        width: 1
    }
}
```

This code will set the animation duration for the marker's movement to 100 milliseconds and change its color to red. The `width` property determines the size of the marker.

Fine-tuning the appearance

The data points in the heat map don't transition through colors, nor do they show data labels. If you would like to make them and their values more prominent, we can achieve it by setting the border and enabling data labels on the series:

```
series: [{
    name: 'Temperature',
    borderWidth: 1,
    borderColor: 'rgba(255, 255, 255, 0.3)',
    dataLabels: {
        enabled: true,
        style: {
            color: '#fff',
            'font-family': 'arial, helvetica, sans-serif',
            'font-size': '12px'
        }
    },
    data: [...]
}]
```

This will produce the following result:

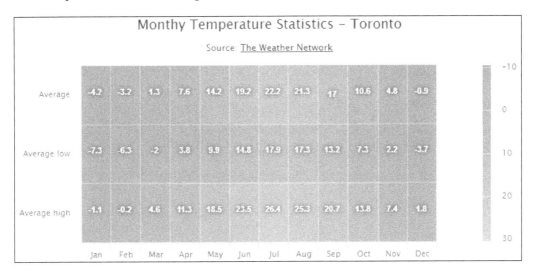

Formatting the tooltip

The default tooltip for the preceding heat map does not display data in the correct format:

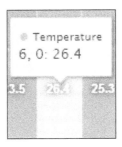

The data we need in the tooltip is the axes' value and the value of the data point. We can fix it by utilizing the `formatter()` method that we used in *Chapter 3*, *Line and Spline Charts*.

```
tooltip: {
    useHTML: true,
    formatter: function() {
        return '<strong>' + this.series.yAxis.categories[this.point.y]
+ '</strong><br /><strong>' + this.series.xAxis.categories[this.
point.x] + ':</strong> ' + this.point.value + '&deg;C';
    }
}
```

Since we needed to show the respective categories of both the axes upon hovering over a data point, we accessed the categories array on the axes by `this.series.xAxis.categories` and `this.series.yAxis.categories`. For the correct element (category name) to show, we determined the index by `this.point.x` and `this.point.y` for xAxis and yAxis respectively. We then formatted the markup with simple HTML and returned the modified value.

The preceding code will produce the following result:

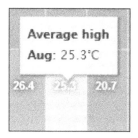

Summary

In this chapter, we explored different Highcharts types. We first learned about different gauges, including the angular gauge, solid gauge, and VU meter. We modified their appearance, including their pane and background, by utilizing their different configuration options. Then we explored waterfall, pyramid, and funnel charts. At the end, we learned about heat maps, a new chart type added to Highcharts Version 4.

This concludes our journey exploring chart types that come with Highcharts. In the next chapter, we will begin working with the theming API to overhaul the appearance of our charts.

7
Theming with Highcharts

Besides the charting capabilities offered by Highcharts, theming is yet another strong feature of Highcharts. With its extensive theming API, charts can be customized completely to match the branding of a website or an app. Almost all of the chart elements are customizable through this API. While we have taken a look at some of the theming options in the earlier chapters, such as margins, offsets, and font variations, in this chapter we will explore the theming API in more details. We will do the following things:

- Familiarize ourselves with basic theming concepts
- Customize different Highcharts elements
- Use different fill types and fonts
- Create a global theme for our charts
- Use jQuery easing for animations
- Configure our charts for RTL

We can breakdown theming into two parts:

- **Layout**: This includes margins, paddings, and offsets
- **Style**: This includes all the fancy stuff such as colors, shadows, gradients, strokes, fonts, animations, and so on

We will look exclusively at both of the above in the current chapter.

Basic theming concepts

Before we move on to theming Highcharts, let's recall that all the options in Highcharts are given in hierarchical structure. This concept also applies to theming with Highcharts. If we need to style any component, we can define those styles within that component. Individual components in different series can have different styles. This ability to define formatting and style on both the global and series level gives us more control and flexibility over the aesthetics of the charts.

By default, Highcharts has predefined colors for series defined in an array:

```
colors: ['#7cb5ec', '#434348', '#90ed7d', '#f7a35c', '#8085e9',
'#f15c80', '#e4d354', '#8085e8', '#8d4653', '#91e8e1']
```

Highcharts applies these colors to the series in sequential order. When all the colors are used, they are pulled from the start of the array again.

We will modify an example of a combination of different chart types from *Chapter 5, Pie, Polar, and Spider Web Charts*, to define our custom colors for series in the `series` object:

```
{
  ...
  colors: ['#75C7F5', '#86A667', '#EEA237', '#D9514E', '#282826',
'#F2D06B'],
  ...
}
```

This modification to code will give the following result:

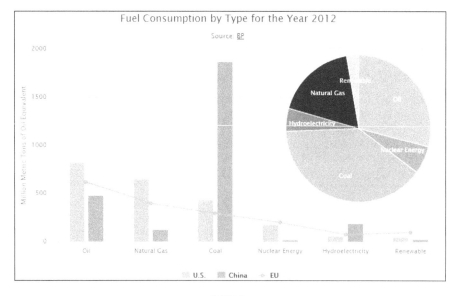

The preceding screenshot shows how Highcharts applies colors defined in the `colors` array to all of the series regardless of their type.

If we were to apply these colors to only a specific series type, for example, column, then we would have done that by defining the color array inside `plotOptions.column`:

```
column: {
  colors: ['#75C7F5', '#86A667', '#EEA237', '#D9514E', '#282826',
'#F2D06B'],
  colorByPoint: true
}
```

In the preceding code, we set the `colorByPoint` property to `true`. By default, colors are applied on a per-series basis, that is, one color per series. The `colorByPoint` property determines whether the series should receive one color per point, as defined in the `colors` array. Hence, each point would have its separate color.

This will apply the defined colors only to series of type `column`:

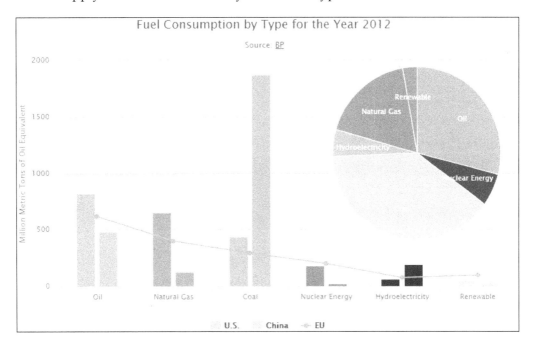

Each column of the series will be colored as per the respective element in the `colors` array. When all of the colors are used, color assignment will be started from the start of the array again.

Alternatively, we could also define the colors array on an individual series using the same code, thus distinguishing it from the rest of its counterparts:

```
[{
  ...
  colors: [...],
  ...
}, {
  ...
  colors: [...],
  ...
},
...]
```

This modification to code will give the following result:

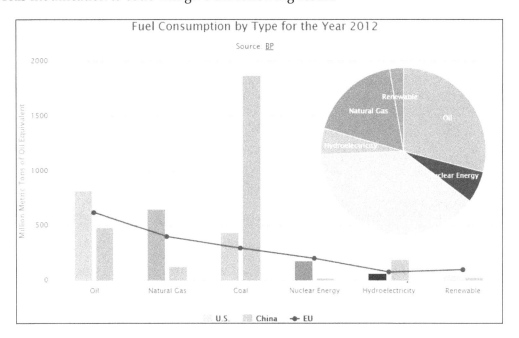

The purpose of all the preceding code was to demonstrate the flexibility of the Highcharts theming API that allows us to define style and formatting on multiple levels of hierarchy. In the next section, we will dive even further into this API by customizing the default tooltip. We will define the layout by HTML and the styling by CSS, all using the Highcharts API.

Formatting the tooltip with HTML

In the previous chapter, we wrote a considerably large amount of code to modify the output of the tooltip. In this section, we will take that knowledge even further by introducing the country names in the tooltip, using as an example the Olympics medal table from *Chapter 2, Column and Bar Charts*.

A simple thing we can start with is to change each series color based on the type of medal it represents, as shown in the following code:

```
series: [{
  name: 'Gold',
  data: [46, 38, 24, 29, 13],
  color: '#cc9900'
}, {
  name: 'Silver',
  data: [29, 27, 26, 17, 8],
  color: '#cccccc'
}, {
  name: 'Bronze',
  data: [29, 23, 32, 19, 7],
  color: '#cd7f32'
}]
```

The preceding code will give the following result:

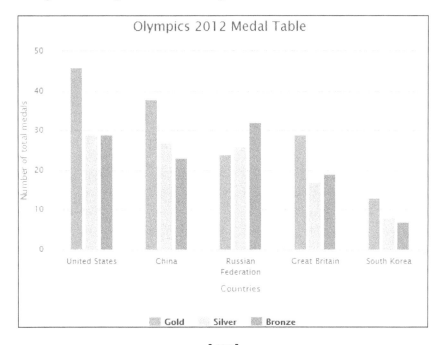

We can now actually begin with the tooltip customization. I have downloaded the flags of the plotted countries and have put them inside the img folder. We will first check for the country that is being hovered — the category at the xAxis. Based on country, we will show the respective flag along with other formatting:

```
tooltip: {
  formatter: function() {
    var img = '',
      string = '';
    if ( 'United States' == this.x ) {
      img = 'img/usa.png';
    } else if ( 'China' == this.x ) {
      img = 'img/china.png';
    } else if ( 'Russian Federation' == this.x ) {
      img = 'img/russia.png';
    } else if ( 'Great Britain' == this.x ) {
      img = 'img/uk.png';
    } else if ( 'South Korea' == this.x ) {
      img = 'img/korea.png';
    }
      return '<img src="' + img + '" alt="' + this.x + '" />';
  }
  useHTML: true
}
```

We used the same formatter() method that we have used in the previous chapters. Inside that method, we initialized two variables, img and string, to hold the flag image path and the final HTML string respectively. After that, we ran some conditions to determine the current xAxis category, that is, the country so that we could assign the img variable path to the correct flag. Finally, an HTML image tag containing the country flag has been returned to ensure that things are working the way they should be, as shown in the following screenshot:

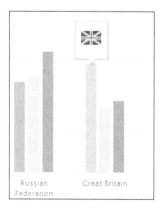

If you hover over any column, the country flag will be shown in the tooltip based on the current *x* axis category.

It's time to include some more HTML to define the proper structure of the tooltip, as using the `formatter()` method completely overrides the default formatting:

```
string += '<div class="country-flag"><img src="' + img + '" alt="' +
this.x + '" /></div>';
string += '<div class="medal-info">';
string += '<h4>' + this.x + '</h4>';
string += '<p><span class="medal-circle" style="background:' + this.
series.color + '"></span>' + this.series.name + ': ' + this.y + '</
p>';
string += '</div>';
return string;
```

That's a pretty simple HTML structure. Instead of returning a simple string containing the image element, we are appending the HTML code, bit by bit, to the `string` variable to return it at the end. The flag image is contained in a `div` tag of class `country-flag` and the other information is enclosed in a `div` tag of class `medal-info`. We referenced the country name and its medal count using `this.x` and `this.y`, respectively. For determining the series name, that is, the medal type, we have used the `this.series.name` property.

For showing a medal before the medal count, we used a `span` tag of the class `medal-circle`. To show the proper color, we added the `style` attribute to define its background color, whose value is determined by the `this.series.color` property.

General styling of all these tags is defined in the page header inside the `style` tag:

```
.country-flag {
  display: inline-block;
  margin-right: 6px;
  vertical-align: top;
}

.medal-info {
  font-family: arial, helvetica, sans-serif;
  font-size: 12px;
  display: inline-block;
}

.medal-circle {
  display: inline-block;
  width: 8px;
  height: 8px;
```

```
    border-radius: 12px;
    margin-right: 4px;
}

.medal-info h4 {
    font-weight: bold;
    color: #222222;
    margin: 0 0 6px;
}

.medal-info p {
    margin: 0 0 6px;
}
```

All of this code will create a nicely formatted tooltip:

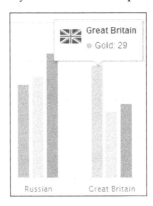

The most important point we learned by following this example is that we can define our own markup for various Highcharts components, and define their styling based on their class names outside of the Highcharts API.

Altering borders, shadows, and backgrounds

In this section, we will look at some of the Highcharts options that are available to modify borders, shadows, and backgrounds. Continuing with the previous example, we will add some more styling for the tooltip. However, instead of using CSS, this time we will utilize the options provided by Highcharts:

```
tooltip: {
    ...
    useHTML: true,
```

```
    backgroundColor: 'rgba(213, 226, 237, 0.6)',
    borderColor: '#eb454d',
    borderRadius: 8,
    borderWidth: 2,
    shadow: false
}
```

By default, `backgroundColor` is `rgba(255, 255, 255, 0.85)` and `borderColor` has the same color as the series. Since we have defined them explicitly, these values will override the default values.

The `borderRadius` and `borderWidth` elements define the radius and width of the border respectively and have values of `3` and `1` by default. We have disabled the shadow by setting it to false.

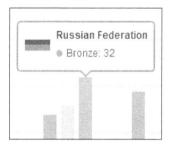

In addition to solid color backgrounds, Highcharts also support linear and radial gradients on a number of components. We will explore gradients along with other fill types in the next section.

Gradient fill types

Currently, the background of the chart is a solid white color. We can have a gradient of either linear or radial type as the background of the chart. Gradients in Highcharts have syntax similar to that of gradients in SVG.

In this section, we will apply gradient fill to various chart components, including the chart itself, series columns, and tooltips.

Linear gradients

To apply a linear gradient on any chart component, we need to define two objects inside the `backgroundColor` property. These two objects are `linearGradient` and `stops`. The `linearGradient` object defines the direction and shape of the gradient, while `stops` defines color transitions and their positions within the gradient.

Consider the following code to define a linear gradient on the chart background:

```
chart: {
  ...
  backgroundColor: {
    linearGradient: {x1: 0, y1: 0, x2: 1, y2: 0},
    stops: [
      [0, '#ffffff'],
      [1, '#ede8d5']
    ]
  }
}
```

The `linearGradient` object holds an object literal containing the coordinates of two points to determine the direction of the gradient. A value of 0 represents the top/left and a value of 1 represents the bottom/right corners. Since we have given the coordinates of (0, 0) and (1, 0), the gradient will start at the top-left corner and will end at the top-right corner of the chart. The same value for *y* coordinates of both the points implies that the gradient will be horizontal in direction.

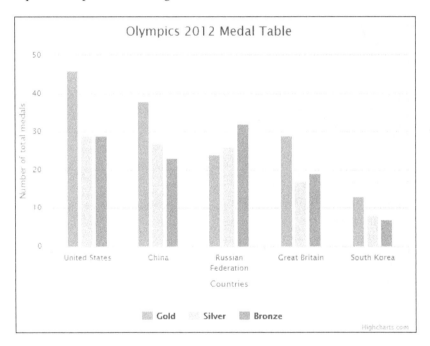

If we were to start the gradient from the top-right corner and end at the bottom-left corner, then we would define the `linearGradient` object as follows:

```
linearGradient: {x1: 1, y1: 0, x2: 0, y2: 1}
```

This modification will result in the following chart:

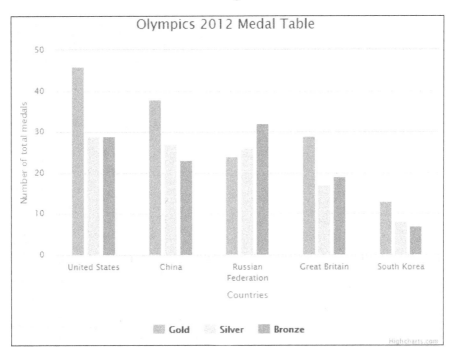

Gradient background for columns and tooltips

We can change the background of tooltips and series columns to include a linear gradient, as shown in the following code:

```
tooltip: {
  ...
  backgroundColor: {
    linearGradient: {x1: 0, y1: 1, x2: 1, y2: 0},
    stops: [
      [0, '#cfd9e3'],
      [1, '#ffffff']
    ]
  }
},
series: [{
  ...
  color: {
    linearGradient: {x1: 0, y1: 0, x2: 1, y2: 0},
```

```
        stops: [
          [0, '#e5ac00'],
          [1, '#cc9900']
        ]
      }
    }, {
      ...
      color: {
        linearGradient: {x1: 0, y1: 0, x2: 1, y2: 0},
        stops: [
          [0, '#cccccc'],
          [1, '#bfbfbf']
        ]
      }
    }, {
      ...
      color: {
        linearGradient: {x1: 0, y1: 0, x2: 1, y2: 0},
        stops: [
          [0, '#e58e37'],
          [1, '#cd7f32']
        ]
      }
    }]
```

This code gives the following result:

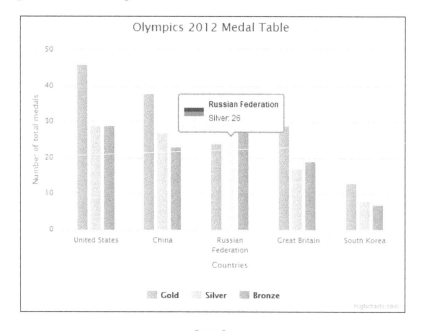

Linear gradients with multiple color stops

We can also define as many color `stops` as we need by specifying their proper positions within the gradient. The following code will include two more color `stops` at various positions in the gradient of the chart background:

```
chart: {
  type: 'column',
  backgroundColor: {
    linearGradient: {x1: 1, y1: 0, x2: 0, y2: 1},
    stops: [
      [0, '#ffffff'],
      [0.4, '#d5edd6'],
      [0.8, '#ede8d5'],
      [1, '#edd5d5']
    ]
  }
}
```

The following is the resultant gradient with four color stops:

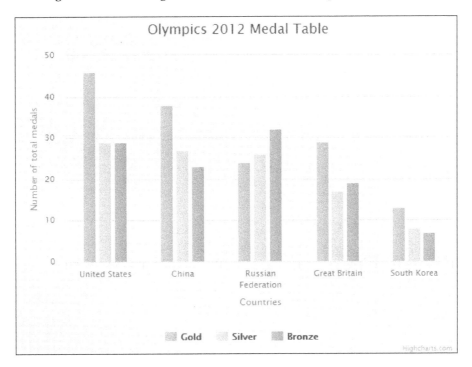

Radial gradients

Radial gradients have syntax similar to linear gradients. The difference is the radius of the gradient and the coordinates of its center point.

In the following code, we will modify the previous example and convert the linear gradient into a radial one:

```
backgroundColor: {
  radialGradient: {cx: 0, cy: 0.9, r: 1},
  stops: [
    [0, '#ffffff'],
    [0.4, '#d5edd6'],
    [0.8, '#ede8d5'],
    [1, '#edd5d5']
  ]
}
```

The cx and cy are the *x* and *y* coordinates of the center of the gradient relative to the shape to which the gradient is being applied. The r property defines the radius of the gradient relative to the shape. A value of 1 means that the gradient will have a radius equal to the size of the shape. In the preceding code, cx being 0 means that the center point of the gradient will be 0 percent from the left along the horizontal. The cy coordinate, with value 0.9, places the gradient's center point at 90 percent from the top. The following is the screenshot of the produced radial gradient:

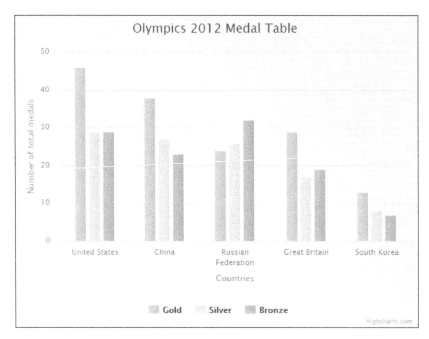

Applying radial gradient to pie chart

When applying radial gradients to pie slices, the position of the gradient is determined relative to the whole circle instead of an individual pie chart. We can apply a radial gradient to a pie chart by passing it in the `colors` array.

Consider the example from the *Chapter 5, Pie, Polar, and Spider Web Charts*, plotting the MS Windows market share via a pie chart. The `plotOptions.pie.colors` array is modified as follows to include radial gradients to pie slices:

```
colors: [{
  radialGradient: {cx: 0.5, cy: 0.5, r: 0.5},
  stops: [
    [0, '#c92121'],
    [1, '#991818']
  ]
}, {
  radialGradient: {cx: 0.5, cy: 0.5, r: 0.5},
  stops: [
    [0, '#cc9621'],
    [1, '#997018']
  ]
}, {
  radialGradient: {cx: 0.5, cy: 0.5, r: 0.5},
  stops: [
    [0, '#65cc21'],
    [1, '#4c9918']
  ]
}, {
  radialGradient: {cx: 0.5, cy: 0.5, r: 0.5},
  stops: [
    [0, '#2185cc'],
    [1, '#186399']
  ]
}, {
  radialGradient: {cx: 0.5, cy: 0.5, r: 0.5},
  stops: [
    [0, '#216ecc'],
    [1, '#185299']
  ]
}]
```

Instead of passing solid colors in the `colors` array, we passed a bunch of object literals holding radial gradients. It will affect the pie chart as shown in the following screenshot:

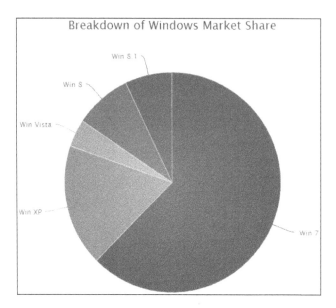

As shown in the preceding screenshot, the radial gradient is starting from 50 percent of the chart, that is, from the middle of the chart. The modification of coordinates on an individual gradient will still position the gradient relative to the circle instead of the pie chart with that gradient.

Using Google Fonts with Highcharts

Google provides an easy way to include hundreds of high quality web fonts to web pages. These fonts work in all major browsers and are served by Google CDN for lightning fast delivery. These fonts can also be used with Highcharts to further polish the appearance of our charts.

 This section assumes that you know the basics of using Google Web Fonts. If you are not familiar with them, visit `https://developers.google.com/fonts/docs/getting_started`.

In the following example, we will take code from the speedometer example from *Chapter 6, Other Chart Types,* to further style it with Google Fonts.

We will use the `Merriweather` family from Google Fonts and link to its style sheet from our web page inside the `<head>` tag:

```
<link href='http://fonts.googleapis.com/css?family=Merriweather:400ita
lic,700italic' rel='stylesheet' type='text/css'>
```

Having included the style sheet, we can actually use the font family in our code for the labels in `yAxis`:

```
yAxis: [{
  ...
  labels: {
    style: {
      fontFamily: 'Merriweather, sans-serif',
      fontWeight: 400,
      fontStyle: 'italic',
      fontSize: '14px',
      color: '#ffffff'
    }
  }
}, {
  ...
  labels: {
    style: {
      fontFamily: 'Merriweather, sans-serif',
      fontWeight: 700,
      fontStyle: 'italic',
      fontSize: '21px',
      color: '#ffffff'
    },
    ...
  }
}]
```

For the outer axis, we used a font size of `21px` with font weight of `700`. For the inner axis, we lowered the font size to `14px` and used font weight of `400` to compensate for the smaller font size.

The following is the modified speedometer:

In the next section, we will continue with the same example to include jQuery UI easing in chart animations.

Using jQuery UI easing for series animation

Animations occurring at the point of initialization of charts can be disabled or customized. The customization requires modifying two properties: `animation.duration` and `animation.easing`. The `duration` property accepts the number of milliseconds for the duration of the animation. The `easing` property can have various values depending on the framework currently being used. For a standalone jQuery framework, the values can be either `linear` or `swing`. Using the jQuery UI framework adds a couple of more options for the `easing` property to choose from.

In order to follow this example, you must include the jQuery UI framework to the page. You can also grab the standalone easing plugin from `http://gsgd.co.uk/sandbox/jquery/easing/` and include it inside your `<head>` tag.

We can now modify the series to have a modified animation:

```
plotOptions: {
  ...
  series: {
    animation: {
      duration: 1000,
```

```
           easing: 'easeOutBounce'
         }
       }
     }
   }
```

The preceding code will modify the `animation` property for all the series in the chart to have `duration` set to `1000` milliseconds and easing to `easeOutBounce`. Each series can have its own different animation by defining the animation property separately for each series as follows:

```
series: [{
  ...
  animation: {
    duration: 500,
    easing: 'easeOutBounce'
  }
}, {
  ...
  animation: {
    duration: 1500,
    easing: 'easeOutBounce'
  }
}, {
  ...
  animation: {
     duration: 2500,
    easing: 'easeOutBounce'
  }
}]
```

Different animation properties for different series can pair nicely with column and bar charts to produce visually appealing effects.

Creating a global theme for our charts

A Highcharts theme is a collection of predefined styles that are applied before a chart is instantiated. A theme will be applied to all the charts on the page after the point of its inclusion, given that the styling options have not been modified within the chart instantiation. This provides us with an easy way to apply custom branding to charts without the need to define styles over and over again.

In the following example, we will create a basic global theme for our charts. This way, we will get familiar with the fundamentals of Highcharts theming and some API methods.

We will define our theme inside a separate JavaScript file to make the code reusable and keep things clean. Our theme will be contained in an options object that will, in turn, contain styling for different Highcharts components.

Consider the following code placed in a file named custom-theme.js. This is a basic implementation of a Highcharts custom theme that includes colors and basic font styles along with some other modifications for axes:

```
Highcharts.customTheme = {

    colors: ['#1BA6A6', '#12734F', '#F2E85C', '#F27329', '#D95D30',
'#2C3949', '#3E7C9B', '#9578BE'],

    chart: {
        backgroundColor: {
            radialGradient: {cx: 0, cy: 1, r: 1},
            stops: [
                [0, '#ffffff'],
                [1, '#f2f2ff']
            ]
        },
        style: {
            fontFamily: 'arial, sans-serif',
            color: '#333'
        }
    },
    title: {
        style: {
            color: '#222',
            fontSize: '21px',
            fontWeight: 'bold'
        }
    },
    subtitle: {
        style: {
            fontSize: '16px',
            fontWeight: 'bold'
        }
    },
    xAxis: {
        lineWidth: 1,
        lineColor: '#cccccc',
        tickWidth: 1,
        tickColor: '#cccccc',
        labels: {
```

```
                style: {
                    fontSize: '12px'
                }
            }
        },
        yAxis: {
            gridLineWidth: 1,
            gridLineColor: '#d9d9d9',
            labels: {
                style: {
                    fontSize: '12px'
                }
            }
        },
        legend: {
            itemStyle: {
                color: '#666',
                fontSize: '9px'
            },
            itemHoverStyle:{
                color: '#222'
            }
        }
    };
    Highcharts.setOptions( Highcharts.customTheme );
```

We start off by modifying the `Highcharts` object to include an object literal named `customTheme` that contains styles for our charts. Inside `customTheme`, the first option we defined is for series colors. We passed an array containing eight colors to be applied to series. In the next part, we defined a radial gradient as a background for our charts and also defined the default font family and text color. The next two object literals contain basic font styles for the `title` and `subtitle` components.

Then comes the styles for the *x* and *y* axes. For the `xAxis`, we define `lineColor` and `tickColor` to be #cccccc with the `lineWidth` value of 1. The `xAxis` component also contains the font style for its labels.

The *y* axis gridlines appear parallel to the *x* axis that we have modified to have the width and color at 1 and #d9d9d9 respectively.

Inside the `legend` component, we defined styles for the normal and mouse hover states. These two states are stated by `itemStyle` and `itemHoverStyle` respectively. In normal state, the legend will have a color of #666 and font size of 9px. When hovered over, the color will change to #222.

In the final part, we set our theme as the default Highcharts theme by using an API method `Highcharts.setOptions()`, which takes a settings object to be applied to Highcharts; in our case, it is `customTheme`.

The styles that have not been defined in our custom theme will remain the same as the default theme. This allows us to partially customize a predefined theme by introducing another theme containing different styles.

In order to make this theme work, include the file `custom-theme.js` after the `highcharts.js` file:

```
<script src="js/highcharts.js"></script>
<script src="js/custom-theme.js"></script>
```

The output of our custom theme is as follows:

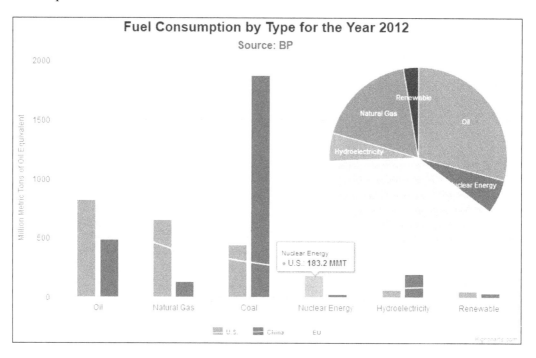

We can also tell our theme to include a web font from Google without having the need to include the style sheet manually in the header, as we did in a previous section. For that purpose, Highcharts provides a utility method named `Highcharts.createElement()`. We can use it as follows by placing the code inside the `custom-theme.js` file:

```
Highcharts.createElement( 'link', {
```

```
    href: 'http://fonts.googleapis.com/css?family=Open+Sans:300italic,
400italic,700italic,400,300,700',
    rel: 'stylesheet',
    type: 'text/css'
}, null, document.getElementsByTagName( 'head' )[0], null );
```

The first argument is the name of the tag to be created. The second argument takes an object as tag attributes. The third argument is for CSS styles to be applied to this element. Since there is no need for CSS styles on a link element, we passed `null` as its value. The final two arguments are for the parent node and padding, respectively.

We can now change the default font family for our charts to `'Open Sans'`:

```
chart: {
    ...
    style: {
        fontFamily: "'Open Sans', sans-serif",
        ...
    }
}
```

The specified Google web font will now be loaded every time a chart with our custom theme is initialized, hence eliminating the need to manually insert the required font style sheet inside the `<head>` tag.

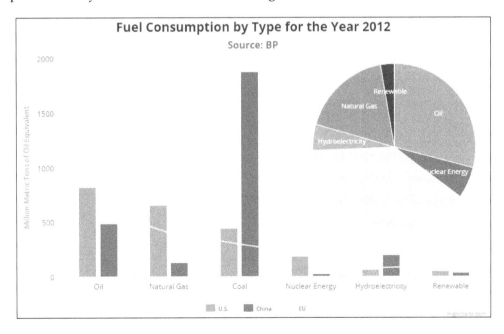

This image shows a chart with `'Open Sans'` Google web font.

Configuring our charts for internationalization

Highcharts can display bidirectional text using SVG capabilities of major modern browsers. However, issues can arise when displaying complex HTML strings in SVG. Therefore, all the text options in Highcharts are accompanied by the useHTML property, used extensively in this book.

Along with displaying bidirectional text, it's also essential to flip the position of the y axis and change the flow of the x axis so that the categories appear from right to left. For this purpose, Highcharts provides properties on both axes, namely xAxis. reversed and yAxis.opposite, which can change the geometry of the chart.

We will continue with the following example to replace English text with Arabic text and change the position and flow of both axes. To translate the text into Arabic, we will use Google Translate (https://translate.google.com).

Observe the following code for chart initialization; we will replace the text with Arabic and change the position of the y axis using the opposite:true property. The reversed property causes the x axis to list categories from right to left, hence changing the direction of text to RTL. The code is as follows:

```
$( '#chart_container' ).highcharts({
  title: {
    text: 'الاستهلاك الوقود حسب نوع لعام 2012'
  },
  subtitle: {
    text: 'مصدر: BP',
    useHTML: true
    },
xAxis: {
    reversed: true,
     categories: ['الطاقة ', 'نووية طاقة ', 'فحم', 'طاقة طبيعي', 'غاز زيت'],
كهرومائية ', 'قابل للتجديد']
  },
  yAxis: {
    opposite: true,
     title: {
    text: 'مليون طن متر من النفط أي ما يعادل'
    }
  },
  plotOptions: {
    pie: {
```

```
        dataLabels: {
          distance: -45,
          color: '#ffffff'
        }
      }
    },
    tooltip: {
      valueSuffix: ' MMT',
      useHTML: true
    },
    series: [{
      name: 'أمريكا',
      type: 'column',
      data: [819.9, 654, 437.4, 183.2, 63.2, 50.7]
    }, {
      name: 'الصين',
      type: 'column',
      data: [483.7, 129.5, 1873.3, 22, 194.8, 31.9]
    }, {
      name: 'الاتحاد الأوروبي',
      type: 'line',
      data: [618.8, 399.7, 293.4, 199.9, 76.1, 97.7]
    }, {
      name: 'مجموع',
      type: 'pie',
      data: [
        {name: 'زيت', y: 1922.4},
        {name: 'طاقة نووية', y: 405.1},
        {name: 'فحم', y: 2604.1},
        {name: 'الطاقة الكهرومائية', y: 334.1},
        {name: 'غاز طبيعي', y: 1183.2},
        {name: 'قابل للتجديد', y: 180.3}
      ],
      size: '80%',
      center: ['20%', '40%']
    }]
});
```

Note the use of the useHTML property on the tooltip. This enables the tooltip to have proper RTL text when it is styled through CSS using its default class:

```
.highcharts-tooltip {
  direction: rtl;
}
```

We also changed the position of the pie series within the chart to `['20%', '40%']` so that it appears left-aligned.

The following screenshot is of the chart resulting from the preceding code:

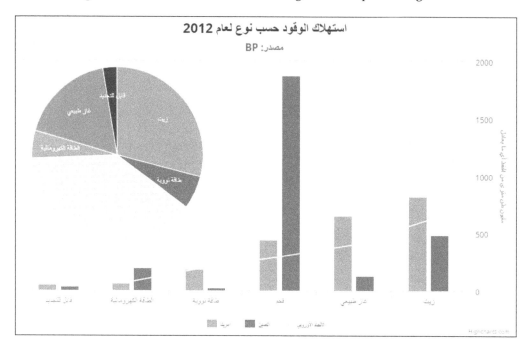

Summary

In this chapter, we took a detailed look at theming Highcharts using its API and CSS. We formatted the tooltip using HTML to include an image and used CSS to give it a brand new look. Then we modified its borders, backgrounds, and shadows using the API. Then, you learned about gradients and how we can use them as background for chart and other components. You then learned about incorporating Google fonts and jQuery UI easing into our chart for enhanced styling. Then, a custom theme was created that could be used for multiple charts across the website or web app. Finally, we configured our chart to show RTL text.

In the next chapter, we will look at Highcharts API and its events in greater detail. This will allow us to programmatically accomplish various tasks.

8
Exploring Highcharts APIs and Events

As developers, we often deal with scenarios where some task needs to be accomplished programmatically. When speaking about Highcharts, these scenarios can be either inserting a new series into an already initialized chart, updating an axis, or destroying a chart on a user-generated event. This is where Highcharts APIs come in handy as they provide us with methods, properties, and events to have full control over our code.

We have used some of the API features in earlier chapters such as setting a theme via the `Highcharts.setOptions()` method and using its properties on series to get values on x and y axes. In this chapter, we will examine Highcharts APIs more closely to arm ourselves with necessary skills that will prove useful when working with Highcharts.

However, before pressing on to Highcharts APIs and events, we shall first familiarize ourselves with the Highcharts class model as it's crucial to have a deep understanding of APIs. The class model defines how objects are structured inside a chart, thus letting us maneuver APIs by referring to these objects. And finally, we will look at ways to extend Highcharts to add extra functionality.

In this chapter, we will cover the following topics:

- Familiarizing ourselves with the Highcharts class structure
- Getting to know the essential Highcharts API methods and events
- Looking at how various tasks can be accomplished programmatically
- Learning how to extend Highcharts to add extra functionality

An overview of Highcharts APIs and class model

A Highcharts chart is composed of five different classes namely `Chart`, `Axis`, `Series`, `Point`, and `Renderer`. Each object contains methods to accomplish different tasks and properties that contain vital information about that object. They also contain properties to reference back to higher-level objects, thus allowing access to properties and methods of other objects.

The purpose of each class is listed as follows:

- `Chart`: It is the top-level class that represents the chart. It contains methods, such as `addAxis()`, `addSeries()`, `destroy()`, and `getSVG()` to carry out operations on the chart as a whole. Within this class, there are arrays that contain objects for *x* axis, *y* axis, and series. You can find out more about the `Chart` class, its methods, and properties at `http://api.highcharts.com/highcharts#Chart`.

- `Axis`: This class represents the chart axes. It has methods to deal with axis-specific operations including `getExtremes()` to get extreme values on the axis, `addPlotBand()` to add a plot band, and `setCategories()` to set categories after the chart has been rendered. The `chart` property can be used to refer back to the parent chart object. More information can be found at `http://api.highcharts.com/highcharts#Axis`.

- `Series`: The `Series` class is responsible for managing data points inside a particular series. The `data` array contains all data point objects that are specific to this series. This class includes methods such as `addPoint()` to add a data point after the render time as well as the `hide()` and `show()` methods to hide and show the series, respectively. It also has a `chart` property to refer back to the parent chart object. You can find more about `Series` at `http://api.highcharts.com/highcharts#Series`.

- `Point`: The `Point` class represents a single data point. Its property list includes x and y properties representing its values on each of the axes. The `series` property is used to refer back to the parent series object. The documentation about `Point` object can be found at `http://api.highcharts.com/highcharts#Point`.

- `Renderer`: This class does all the heavy lifting of rendering a chart using SVG or VML in legacy browsers. It has a one-to-one correspondence with each chart and contains methods to draw various shapes. It can also be accessed independently for drawing outside a chart. You can find out more about its methods and properties at `http://api.highcharts.com/highcharts#Renderer`.

Apart from these classes, an `Element` class is used in combination with the `Renderer` class to render SVG elements. Then, there is the `Highcharts` namespace, under which some API functions and variables are assembled.

As mentioned previously, each class object has properties to transverse through the object hierarchy. Consider the example from *Chapter 5, Pie, Polar, and Spider Web Charts*, modified to include a callback function to execute after the chart has been initialized:

```
(function() {
  $( '#chart_container' ).highcharts({
    title: {
      text: 'Fuel Consumption by Type for the Year 2012'
    },
    subtitle: {
      ...
    },
    xAxis: {
      ...
    },
    yAxis: {
      ...
    },
    plotOptions: {
      ...
    },
    tooltip: {
      ...
    },
    series: [
      ...
    ]
  }, function() {
    console.log( this );
  });
})();
```

Inside the callback function, the `this` keyword refers to the top-level `chart` object. Hence, by logging the `this` variable we are executing the contents of the `chart` object:

```
Q   Elements  Network  Sources  Timeline  Profiles  Resources  Audits  Console
⊘  ▽  <top frame>  ▼
  ▼ Ya
      _cursor: ""
      _sharedClip,1000,,360: null
      _sharedClip,1000,,360m: null
      angular: undefined
      animation: true
    ▶ axes: Array[2]
    ▶ axisOffset: Array[4]
    ▶ bounds: Object
    ▶ callback: function () {
      cancelClick: false
    ▶ chartBackground: P
      chartHeight: 500
      chartWidth: 800
    ▶ clipBox: Object
    ▶ clipOffset: Array[4]
  Console  Search  Emulation  Rendering
```

The preceding screenshot shows the contents of the `chart` object logged in Chrome's **Developer Tools**.

> Developer tools provide a great deal of help when debugging web applications within the browser. Every major browser comes with its own plugins; third-party plugins, such as Firebug for Mozilla Firefox are also available. We are using Chrome's **Developers Tools**, about which you can find more at https://developer.chrome.com/devtools.

When inspecting the `chart` object with developer tools, we can access all the methods and properties right within the console. This provides us with a convenient way to play around with APIs without having the need to switch back and forth between the JavaScript (or HTML) file and the browser. To access the `chart` object, we first need to set it as a global variable. To do so, right-click on the top-level object and select the **Store as global variable** option from the context menu:

By doing so, Chrome will copy a reference to the `chart` object to a newly created variable in the global context and output the name of that global variable in the next line, in this case, **temp1**:

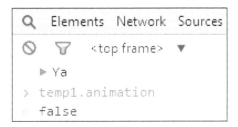

We can now access the properties and methods on the `chart` object by referring to the `temp1` global variable.

Disabling the chart animation

The chart animation property, `chart.animation`, is set to `true` by default. We can use the newly created global variable to turn the animation off by typing the following code in the **Developer Tools** console:

```
temp1.animation = false;
```

We can verify the change either by toggling series by their legends or by outputting the value of the `temp1.animation` property, which will return **false**:

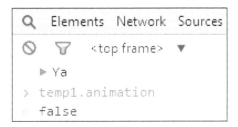

This is one way by which we can navigate through the Highcharts class structure. In the next section, we will look at another way through which we can obtain an axis, series, or a point of a chart.

Getting values with the Chart.get() method

The `Chart.get()` method can be used to get an axis, series, or a point by its ID. It returns an object of an axis, series, or a point containing various properties. This method is useful due to faster access to the mentioned components, as we don't have to manually navigate through the object hierarchy of a chart.

 Note that this method is only available in the top-level chart object.

Consider the following example from *Chapter 7*, *Theming with Highcharts*, modified to include an ID for the Windows 7 data point:

```
$( '#chart_container' ).highcharts({
  chart: {
    type: 'pie'
  },
  title: {
    ...
  },
  tooltip: {
    ...
  },aotOptions: {
    ...
  },
  series: [{
    name: 'Windows versions',
    data: [
      {
        name: 'Win 7',
        id: 'win7',
        y: 55.03
      },
      ...
    ]
  }]
}
```

While being on the top-level `chart` object, we can call the `get()` method in the callback function to get the object of the `win7` data point:

```
var win7Point = this.get( 'win7' );
```

Upon logging the `win7Point` variable in the console, we get the following object:

```
▼ c {series: c, name: "Win 7", id: "win7", y: 55.03, options: Object…}
    angle: 0.38953754016333364
  ► color: Object
  ► connector: P
  ► dataLabel: P
  ► graphic: P
    half: 0
    id: "win7"
  ► jQuery111103055207394063473: Object
  ► labelPos: Array[8]
    name: "Win 7"
  ► options: Object
    percentage: 62.399365007370456
  ► pointAttr: Array[0]
  ► series: c
  ► shapeArgs: Object
    shapeType: "arc"
  ► slicedTranslation: Object
  ► tooltipPos: Array[2]
    total: 88.19
    visible: true
    x: 0
    y: 55.03
  ► __proto__: Ea
```

The `win7Point` object also contains the `series` property, which can be used to navigate upwards in the object hierarchy.

While being tremendously useful, the limitation of the `Chart.get()` method is that it can only be used to retrieve axes, series, or points that have already been assigned an ID.

Adding series and points

We can dynamically add axes, series, and points to any chart after it has been initialized. In the following examples, we will first initialize a chart and then add points and series to it upon different actions.

Adding a point dynamically

Consider the following code for a chart representing energy consumption by leading continents in 2013:

```
(function() {
  $( '#energy_consumption' ).highcharts({
    title: {
      text: 'Energy Consumption in 2013'
    },
    xAxis: {
      type: 'category',
      title: {
        text: 'Continents'
      }
    },
    yAxis: {
      title: {
        text: 'Million Metric Tons of Oil Equivalent'
      }
    },
    series: [{
      name: 'Energy Consumption',
      type: 'column',
      data:  [{
        id: 'north-america',
        name: 'North America',
        y: 2786.7
      }, {
        id: 'asia',
        name: 'Asia',
        y: 5594
      }]
    }]
  });
})();
```

This chart will have two data points for two continents showing their energy consumption bar, that is, North America and Asia, respectively:

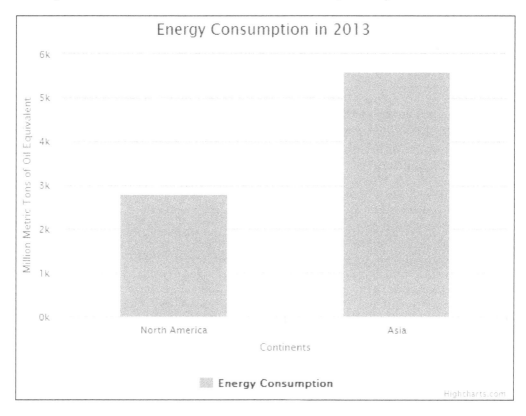

We will now add a button so that when someone clicks on it a new data point for Europe will be added to the series.

Add the following code for the button element:

```
<button data-action="add_europe">Add Europe Data Point</button>
```

Here, we are using HTML5 custom data attributes to define the behavior of the button.

The following is the JavaScript code to add a data point. Add it after the chart's initialization code:

```
var chart = $( '#energy_consumption' ).highcharts(),
addEuropeBtn = $( '[data-action="add_europe"]' );

addEuropeBtn.on( 'click', function( e ) {
```

```
    if ( ! chart.get( 'europe' ) ) {
      chart.series[0].addPoint({
        id: 'europe',
        name: 'Europe',
        y: 1286.1
      });
    }
  });
```

We first saved a reference to the initialized chart in the `chart` variable and also cached a reference to the button in the `addEuropeBtn` variable. Then, using the jQuery `.on()` method, we added an anonymous function to be executed upon a click event of the button.

Inside the function, we added a condition to check whether the Europe data point has already been added to the series by the `chart.get()` method. If the data point has not been added yet, it will return as `null`. The condition will pass since the negation of `null` is `true` and a point will be added to the first series, that is, `series[0]`, using the `series.addPoint()` method.

Inside the `series.addPoint()` method, we have passed an object literal containing the `id`, `name`, and `y` value of the data point.

By clicking on the button, a new point will be added and the chart will be redrawn:

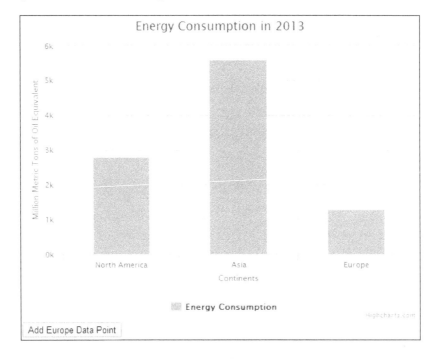

When adding multiple points at once, it's recommended to set the redraw argument of the `addPoint()` method to `false` and call the `chart.redraw()` method explicitly after the point addition, as shown in the following generic code:

```
Button.on( 'click', function( e ) {
  chart.series[i].addPoint({...}, false);
  chart.series[i].addPoint({...}, false);
  chart.series[i].addPoint({...}, false);
  chart.redraw();
});
```

You can find more about the `chart.addPoint()` method by visiting the following link on Highcharts documentation:

```
http://api.highcharts.com/highcharts#Series.addPoint
```

In the next section, we will look at adding a series dynamically to a chart.

Adding a series dynamically

Similar to a point, a series can also be added to a chart after it has been initialized. This is achieved by utilizing the `chart.addSeries()` method that accepts a series object as its first argument.

Continuing with the previous example, we will now add a button to add a new series of type, `pie`. The HTML code for the button is as follows:

```
<button data-action="add_pie">Add Pie Series</button>
```

Clicking on this button will create a new array of arrays, each containing a pair of series `name` and its `y` value. This array will be used as data for the newly added series:

```
var addPieSeriesBtn = $( '[data-action="add_pie"]' ),
pieSeriesData = [];

addPieSeriesBtn.on( 'click', function( e ) {

  if ( ! chart.get( 'percentage' ) ) {
    for ( var i in chart.series[0].data ) {
      pieSeriesData.push( [chart.series[0].data[i].name,
      chart.series[0].data[i].y] );
    }

    var pieSeries = {
```

```
            name: 'Percentage',
            id: 'percentage',
            type: 'pie',
            data: pieSeriesData,
            center: ['80%', '25%'],
            size: 200,
            tooltip: {
              enabled: false
            },
            dataLabels: {
              color: '#fff',
              distance: -45,
              y: -10,
              useHTML: true,
              formatter: function() {
                return this.point.name + '<br />' +
                this.percentage.toFixed( 2 ) + '%';
              }
            }
          };
        chart.setSize( 800, 450 );
        chart.addSeries( pieSeries );
      }
    });
```

We first gathered the data to be plotted from the series of the initialized chart in the form of an array containing the name and y value of the data points. These arrays will be collected in another array called pieSeriesData.

In the next step, we initialized an object literal containing the properties of the new series. For its data property, we passed the pieSeriesData array. We used the formatter() method to format the output of data labels. This will return the percentages representing each data point with two decimal places. To set the decimal places, we used the native JavaScript method, .toFixed(), that accepts a number representing decimal places.

Finally, we increased the width of the chart using the chart.setSize() method that accepts width and height as its arguments. This will make place for the newly added pie series. The series is added to the chart through the chart.addSeries() method that accepts an object literal containing the properties of the series; in our case, it's pieSeries.

This will produce the following result, given that the Europe data point is already added to the chart:

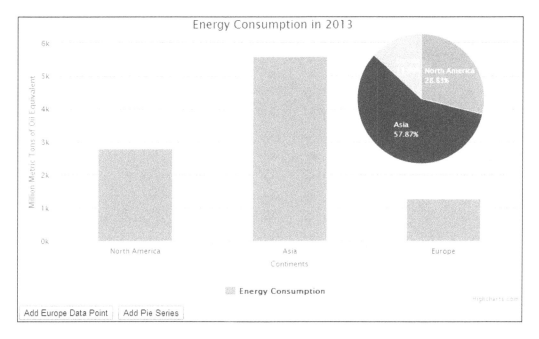

You can find more about the `chart.addSeries()` method at the following link:

`http://api.highcharts.com/highcharts#Chart.addSeries`

Adding drilldowns to series

Now that we have plotted a chart that shows energy consumption data for three continents, we can add drilldown series to these data points showing a share of each country in the respective continent.

For the sake of simplicity, we will remove the pie series for now and pass the Europe data point as a chart configuration object:

```
$( '#energy_consumption' ).highcharts({
  title: {
    ...
  },
  xAxis: {
    ...
  },
  yAxis: {
```

```
      ...
  },
  series: [{
      ...
    data:  [{
      name: 'North America',
        ...
    }, {
      name: 'Asia',
        ...
    }, {
      name: 'Europe',
        ...
    }]
  }]
});
```

Adding drilldown to a point is as simple as adding a series, which we looked at in the previous section. It's accomplished via the `chart.addSeriesAsDrilldown()` method that accepts the `point` object to which the series is being added as its first argument. For the second argument, it accepts the `series` object as the drilldown series.

For simulation purposes, we will create an object containing object literals for all the drilldown series in a key value pair. The key will be the ID of the data point and the value will be an object literal containing the drilldown series. The following code illustrates this:

```
var drilldownSeries = {
  'north-america': {
    type: 'column',
    name: 'North America',
    data: [
      ['U.S', 2265.8],
      ['Mexico', 188],
      ['Canada', 332.9]
    ]
  },
  'asia': {
    type: 'column',
    name: 'Asia',
    data: [
      ['China', 2852.4],
      ['Russian Federation', 699],
```

```
          ['India', 595],
          ['Japan', 474],
          ['South Korea', 271.3],
          ['Iran', 243.9],
          ['Saudi Arabia', 227.7],
          ['Indonesia', 168.7],
          ['Kazakhstan', 62]
        ]
    },
    'europe': {
      type: 'column',
      name: 'Europe',
      data: [
          ['Germany', 311.7],
          ['France', 248.4],
          ['UK', 200],
          ['Italy', 158.8],
          ['Spain', 133.7],
          ['Ukraine', 117.5],
          ['Australia', 116]
        ]
    }
  }
};
```

We also need to set the `drilldown` property to `true` on all the data points in the
`Energy Consumption` series:

```
series: [{
  name: 'Energy Consumption',
  type: 'column',
  data:  [{
      ...
    name: 'North America',
    drilldown: true
  }, {
      ...
    name: 'Asia',
    drilldown: true
  }, {
      ...
    name: 'Europe',
    drilldown: true
  }]
}]
```

Make sure that the page also includes the `drilldown.js` script after the `highcahrts.js` script as it's required for the drilldown functionality to work.

We will now set up a functionality so that, when anyone clicks on a data point, a drilldown series will be added dynamically. In a real world scenario, the page will request the drilldown data from a server asynchronously, but here we are simulating that case by predefining the drilldown data in the form of a `drilldownSeries` object.

Modify the `chart` component in the chart configuration object to include a callback function for the `drilldown` event:

```
chart: {
  events: {
    drilldown: function( e ) {
      this.addSeriesAsDrilldown( e.point,
      drilldownSeries[e.point.id] );
    }
  }
},
```

The callback function accepts the event object as its argument; it contains vital data about the event. When inspected with developer tools, it looks like the following:

```
▼ m.Event
  ▶ currentTarget: Ya
    data: null
  ▶ delegateTarget: Ya
  ▶ handleObj: Object
    isTrigger: 3
    jQuery1111014011681382554434: true
    namespace: ""
    namespace_re: null
  ▶ point: Ea
  ▶ preventDefault: function (){try{c.call(f)}catch(a){b==="preventDefault"&&(h=!0)}}
    result: undefined
    seriesOptions: undefined
  ▶ stopPropagation: function (){try{c.call(f)}catch(a){b==="preventDefault"&&(h=!0)}}
  ▶ target: Ya
    timeStamp: 1408901604770
    type: "drilldown"
  ▶ __proto__: Object
```

Within this event object, an object for the point that has been clicked, that is, `e.point` can be used as a point object when using the `chart.addSeriesAsDrilldown()` method.

To pick up the right series from the `drilldownSeries` object, we used `e.point.id` as an identifier that will match the key of the correct object.

Drilling up to the parent series

A chart can also be drilled up to the parent series programmatically using the `chart.drillUp()` method.

Modify the `drilldown` event in the `chart` component as shown in the following code:

```
chart: {
  events: {
    drilldown: function( e ) {
      var chart = this;
      chart.addSeriesAsDrilldown( e.point,
      drilldownSeries[e.point.id] );
      setTimeout(function() {
        chart.drillUp();
      }, 5000 );
    }
  }
},
```

The chart will drill up to the parent series five seconds after the drilldown.

In the next section, we will look at various ways to set and get properties on a chart.

Accomplishing various tasks programmatically

We might need to alter the existing properties of the chart at various occasions after the initialization. For that purpose, Highcharts provides methods for each of its components. In the following examples, we will change various chart properties using the method that Highcharts provides.

Setting extreme values on an axis

Currently, the extreme values on the `yAxis` component are `0` and `6K`, respectively. We can change them programmatically using the `Axis.setExtremes()` method.

Instead of adding a button in HTML and then setting values upon its click, it will be faster to use the developer tools' console as our playground.

We first need to get a reference to the chart object; we can do so using the following code:

```
var chart = $( '#energy_consumption' ).highcharts();
```

We can now navigate the chart object hierarchy and call various methods using the chart variable:

```
chart.yAxis[0].setExtremes(0, 10000);
```

Since each chart can contain multiple *x* and *y* axes, we used array notation as yAxis[0] to call the setExtremes() method on the first yAxis component.

The extreme values are set on the *y* axis:

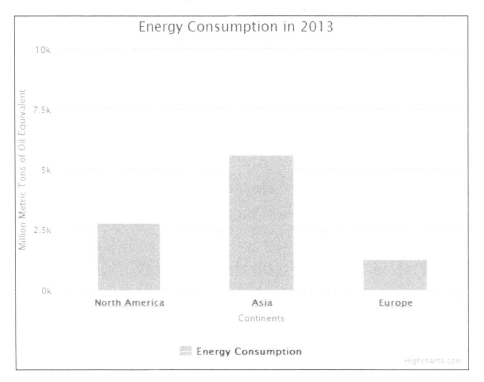

Setting the chart title programmatically

The title of the chart can be changed after it has been initialized. Type the following code in the developer tools' console to set the title to a different one:

```
var chart = $( '#energy_consumption' ).highcharts();
chart.setTitle( {text: prompt('Enter the new title')} );
```

A prompt will appear asking for a new title, and it will set the title to the new one:

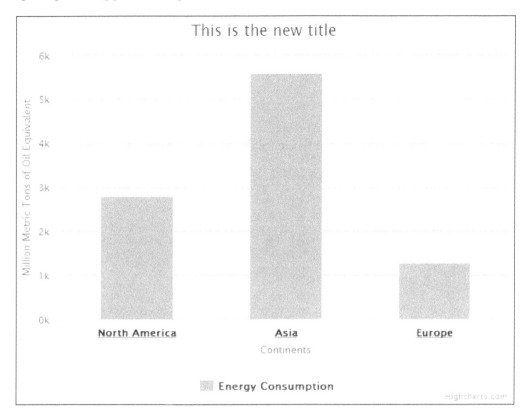

Reflowing a chart

Sometimes the container div is resized without the `window.resize` event, that is, it is resized by JavaScript. In that case, the chart will overflow its parent container. To prevent this problem, the `chart.reflow()` method can be used, which will reflow the chart inside its container.

In the following code, we will first resize the container via jQuery and then call the `chart.reflow()` method to prevent the overflow.

We will add a button for resizing the container and then examine the effect of the `chart.reflow()` method:

```
<button data-action="resize_container">Resize</button>
```

The following code will resize the chart container:

```
$( '[data-action="resize_container"]' ).on( 'click', function( e ) {
  $( '#energy_consumption' ).css({
    width: 400,
    height: 375
  });
});
```

Since we have not called the `chart.reflow()` method yet, the container will resize but the chart will overflow as seen in the following screenshot:

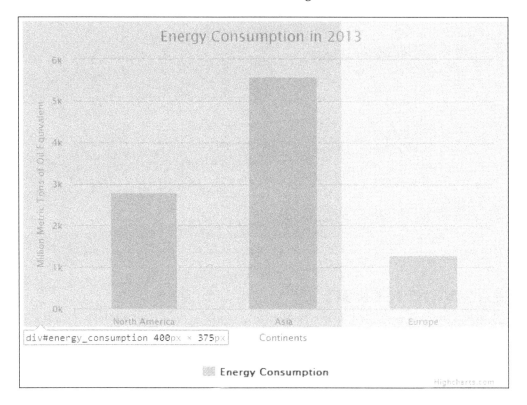

The blue area represents the actual container size that is smaller than the chart size.

Modify the code to include a call to the `chart.reflow()` method as shown in the following code:

```
var chart = $( '#energy_consumption' ).highcharts();
$( '[data-action="resize_container"]' ).on( 'click', function( e ) {
  $( '#energy_consumption' ).css({
    width: 400,
```

```
    height: 375
  });
  chart.reflow();
});
```

Refresh the window and click on the resize button again to see the effect. This time, the container will resize and the chart will be reflowed to fit inside its container:

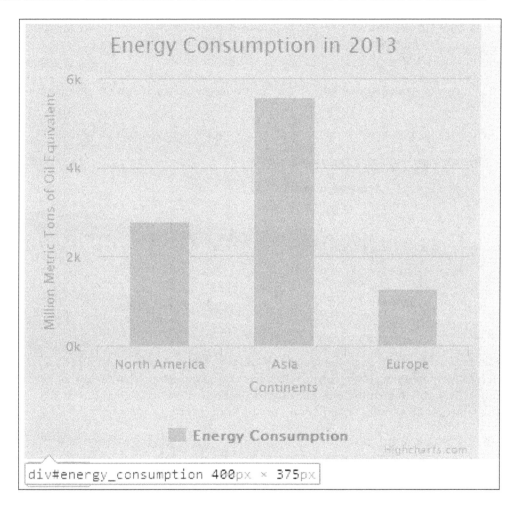

Destroying a chart

When initializing a new chart in the same container, the old chart must be destroyed to empty the container and purge the memory. This method is also called internally on the `window.unload` event to prevent memory leaks.

This method can be called by the following code:

```
chart.destroy();
```

Hiding and showing a series programmatically

A series can be hidden or shown programmatically using the `series.hide()` and `series.show()` methods. In addition to these two methods, the `series.visible` property says whether a series is currently visible or not.

In the following example, we will add a button to toggle a series using the preceding two methods:

```
<button data-action="toggle_series">Toggle Series</button>
```

The code for toggling the series is as follows:

```
var chart = $( '#energy_consumption' ).highcharts(),
  series = chart.series[0];

$( '[data-action="toggle_series"]' ).on( 'click', function( e ) {
  if ( series.visible ) {
    series.hide();
  } else {
    series.show();
  }
});
```

We first saved a reference to the chart and the series in the `chart` and `series` variables, respectively. Then, for the click event of the button we attached a function that will determine whether the series is currently visible and will hide the series. Otherwise, it will show the hidden series.

When toggling a series through a similar API, the series legend will also reflect the change by toggling between the enable and disable state.

In the next section, we will take a look at Highcharts events that occur at various stages in the life span of a chart.

Highcharts events

Highcharts provides seven different events for a chart that are fired at various occasions. These events are as follows:

- `addSeries`: This event is fired when a series is added to the chart after the load time.

- `click`: This event is fired when you click on the plot background of the chart.

- `drilldown`: This event is fired when a data point with drilldown is clicked, but before the drilldown series is added.

- `drillup`: This event is fired when a chart is drilled up to a higher level.

- `load`: This event is fired when a chart has finished loading.

- `redraw`: This event is fired when a chart is redrawn. It also fires when a chart is redrawn by other methods such as `addPoint()` or `addSeries()`.

- `selection`: This event is fired when a point(s) is selected.

The handlers for these events are defined inside the chart component. These handler functions receive an object as an argument that contains information about the event. The event object is defined by the JavaScript library that is being used as Highcharts adapter, for example jQuery or MooTools. In addition to these seven events for the `chart` component, Highcharts also provides events for various other components such as `xAxis`, `yAxis`, and `series.data`. Custom event handlers can also be added to Highcharts for extended functionality. We will look at them in the next section.

You can find more about Highcharts events by visiting the following links:

- `http://api.highcharts.com/highcharts#chart.events`

- `http://api.highcharts.com/highcharts#xAxis.events`

- `http://api.highcharts.com/highcharts#yAxis.events`

- `http://api.highcharts.com/highcharts#series.data.events`

Extending Highcharts

Highcharts has been built in a modular way to help make extending convenient. This capability opens up new possibilities to enhance default functionality. Plugins can be built and custom events can be inserted to account for specific project requirements and client needs.

To extend Highcharts, we wrap our code inside a self-executing anonymous function as follows:

```
(function( H ) {
  //Our code here
})( Highcharts );
```

The function receives an argument, `Highcharts`; this prevents variable pollution in the global scope. In the following example, we will insert a new event handler for the `Point` component.

Adding custom event handlers

In order to add custom event listeners to a chart or its components, we need to push a function to the `Chart.prototype.callbacks` array. This function receives a `chart` object as its argument that can be further used to navigate through chart hierarchy.

In the following example, we will add a custom event handler to the `Point` component to listen for a click event and then remove the point. We will use the `Highcharts.addEvent()` method to register an event handler as follows:

```
(function( H ) {
  H.Chart.prototype.callbacks.push(function( chart ) {
    H.addEvent( chart.series[0].points, 'click', function( e ) {
      e.point.remove();
    });
  });
})( Highcharts );
```

The `addEvent()` method receives an HTML element or a custom object as the first argument and the type of event as the second argument. The final argument is the event handler function that receives an event object as its argument. The event object contains information about the event fired and the corresponding element or the object.

We navigate to the point that has been clicked through `e.point` and call the `Point.remove()` method to remove the point.

Although our function doesn't do much in this case, it should give you a good basis to start experimenting on your own and build some advanced functionality.

Wrapping prototype functions

Sometimes we need to alter the default behavior of the methods that Highcharts uses for its components. We can do so by using the `Highcharts.wrap()` method that accepts the parent object of the method to be altered, the name of the method, and a replacement method, as its arguments, respectively.

In the following code example, we will alter the `hide()` method of the tooltip component that is responsible for hiding the tooltip when the mouse pointer leaves it. We will alter the method to not do anything and hence keep the tooltip always visible.

```
(function( H ) {
  H.wrap( H.Tooltip.prototype, 'hide', function() {
    //do nothing
  });
})( Highcharts );
```

We start by wrapping our code inside the same self-invoking anonymous function. Inside the function, we call the `Highcharts.wrap()` method for the `hide()` method of the tooltip component. We pass an empty function that does nothing and hence keeps the tooltip visible once it's shown.

> You can learn more about extending Highcharts at the following link:
> `http://www.highcharts.com/docs/extending-highcharts/`
> `extending-highcharts`

If you want to learn more about the Highcharts class structure, its components, and methods, then don't be afraid to jump inside the code. The source file we have been using in our examples is the minified one and you can find the actual source in the `Highcharts-4.x.x/js/highcharts.src.js` file.

Summary

In this chapter, we learned about Highcharts APIs, the methods, components, and events it provides to further enhance the functionality. We used Highcharts methods to achieve various tasks programmatically. Then we learned to add custom event handlers to various events and inspected event objects that are passed to event handlers containing vital information.

In the next chapter, we will look at different techniques to load data from different file formats and databases, and will update our chart dynamically using Ajax.

9
Going Further with Highcharts

So far, we have covered different chart types that Highcharts offers as well as their combinations. We have also covered Highcharts APIs and its events that allow us to program interactive charts dynamically. In this chapter, we will cover different techniques to work with data that are essential when developing apps or websites with Highcharts.

Preprocessing data from different file types

When working with a large amount of data, it's not feasible to put all of it on the page itself. Instead, the data is retrieved from an external source such as a file, database, or an API. Before using this data with Highcharts, it's crucial to process it so that it can be plotted correctly. This process of fetching the data and formatting it correctly before it can be plotted is called **preprocessing**.

In the current section, we will take a look at preprocessing data from a number of file formats, including CSV, XML, and JSON. We will also look at JavaScript libraries that make working with these formats easier and also provide a handful of methods to achieve different tasks rather quickly.

Preprocessing data from a CSV file

Comma Separated Values or **Character Separated Values** (CSV) is a common format to store tabular data in plain text. It contains records, each in its own row. These records contain fields separated by a character, usually a comma. It is supported by a number of online and offline applications and is extremely useful when transferring tabular data between programs.

In the following example, we will plot the climate data of Chicago for July, 2014. This data will be presented in a CSV file with three header fields, that is, maximum, minimum, and average temperatures. Each record will correspond to a day in a month except the header record.

Since the parsing of CSV files is not natively supported in JavaScript, we will use an external library **Papa Parse** for this purpose. It's a wonderful library with lots of ground-breaking features such as multi-threaded processing, streaming support, support to parse a string or a file, and JSON-to-CSV conversion. It comes with a handful of useful methods and configuration options. You can find more about Papa Parse and its documentation at `http://papaparse.com/`.

You will need to download Papa Parse and include the `papaparse.min.js` file from the downloaded package into your webpage.

The structure of our webpage stays the same as our previous example, except that we will include an input field of type file to load the CSV file. As soon as the file loads, our callback function will begin parsing the CSV file with Papa Parse and will pass the preprocessed data to the Highcharts configuration object.

The file input field is as follows:

```
<input type="file" id="csv_file">
```

The bare-bone chart configuration object is as follows:

```
var chartConfigOptions = {
  title: {
    text: 'Climate Data for Chicago - July 2014'
  },
  subtitle: {
    text: '<a href="http://www.ncdc.noaa.gov" target="_blank">NCDC</
a>',
    useHTML: true
  },
  chart: {
    type: 'line'
  },
```

```
    tooltip: {
      valueSuffix: '&deg;F',
      useHTML: true
    },
    plotOptions: {
      line: {
        pointStart: Date.UTC(2014, 06, 01, 00, 00, 00),
        pointInterval: 3600 * 1000 * 24
      }
    },
    xAxis: {
      title: {
        text: 'Date'
      },
      type: 'datetime'
    },
    yAxis: {
      title: {
        text: 'Temperature in &deg;F',
        useHTML: true
      }
    },
    series: []
};
```

This is a line chart with xAxis of type datetime to support days of the month. The xAxis component starts at July 1, 2014 and has pointInterval of one day. The series array has been left blank since it will be filled during data preprocessing.

Now, we capture the change event on the file input field and bind a callback function to parse the data in the CSV file:

```
var file = '';
$( '#csv_file' ).on( 'change', function( e ) {
  file = e.target.files[0];
  if ( $( '#climate_data' ).highcharts() ) {
    $( '#climate_data' ).highcharts().destroy();
  }
  Papa.parse( file, {
    header: true,
    complete: function( results ) {
      for ( var i in results.meta.fields ) {
        var name = results.meta.fields[i];
        chartConfigOptions.series[i] = {};
        chartConfigOptions.series[i].name = name;
```

```
          chartConfigOptions.series[i].data = [];
          for ( var j in results.data ) {
            var currentDataPoint = results.data[j][name];
            currentDataPoint = parseInt( currentDataPoint );
            chartConfigOptions.series[i].data.push( currentDataPoint );
          }
        }
        $( '#climate_data' ).highcharts( chartConfigOptions );
      }
    });
  });
```

We first initialize an empty variable `file` for the file DOM object and then bind an event handler to the `change` event on the file input field. Inside the event handler function, the file DOM object is captured with the help of event object `e`.

In the next step, we check whether Highcharts has already been initialized for the same container so the previous chart is destroyed using the `chart.destroy()` method.

In the `Papa.parse()` method, we pass the file DOM object as the first argument and a configuration object containing the callback function as the second argument. Note the use of the `header` property in the configuration object; this will treat the first row of the data that has been passed as field names. Now, each row will be an object of data, keyed by field names. The following are the first three rows of the CSV file:

```
Maximum,Minimum,Average
80,67,74
70,56,63
76,56,66
```

The following screenshot illustrates it as an object in the console:

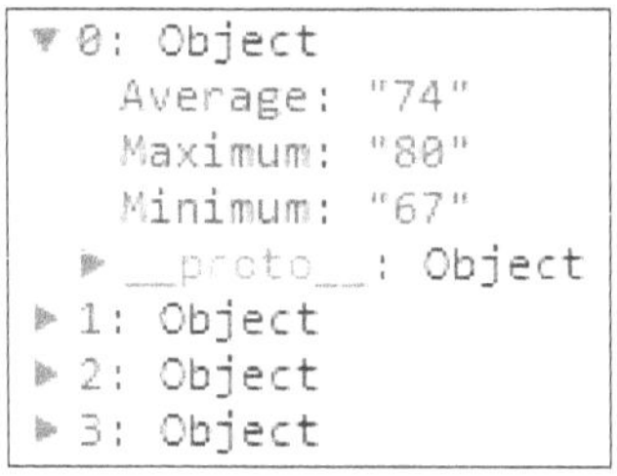

```
▼ 0: Object
    Average: "74"
    Maximum: "80"
    Minimum: "67"
  ▶ __proto__: Object
▶ 1: Object
▶ 2: Object
▶ 3: Object
```

In the next step, the `results.meta.fields` array is looped through, each series is given its name, and an empty array for its `data` is initialized. In an inner loop, the `results.data` array is iterated and fields with the same header field are held into a `currentDataPoint` variable. The `currentDataPoint` variable holds the data point that is currently being iterated. The JavaScript method `parseInt()` is called on the current data point to make sure that it's typecasted as an integer. Finally, the `currentDataPoint` variable is pushed into the `data` array of the current series. This process is repeated for each header field until all the data in the CSV file is processed. Finally, Highcharts is initialized on the container. The following chart is produced with the provided CSV file:

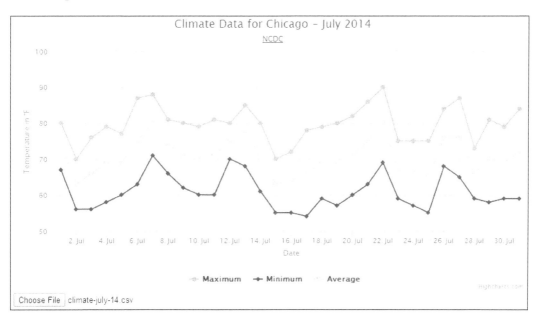

Preprocessing data from an XML file

eXtensible Markup Language (**XML**) is another popular format to save data. It has a similar structure to HTML; in fact, HTML is based on XML. Due to this similar syntax and DOM structure, jQuery can be used to parse XML files.

In the following example, we will plot the same data as we used in the previous example. However, this time the data is saved in XML format. The XML file has data in the following format:

```
<chart>
  <series>
    <name>Maximum</name>
    <points>80,70,76,79,...</points>
```

```
    </series>
    <series>
      ...
    </series>
    <series>
      ...
    </series>
  </chart>
```

As there are no predefined tags in XML, we have defined our own tags to define the markup of our document. The `chart` tag is the top-level tag that contains multiple `series` tags. Each `series` tag has a `name` and `points` tag. The `name` tag contains the name of the series and the `points` tag contains all the data points separated by a comma (,).

The `chartConfigOptions` object used to hold chart configuration options is the same as the previous example. The code to retrieve the XML file and then parsing it is as follows:

```
$.get( 'climate-july-14.xml', function( data ) {
  var xml = $( data );
  xml.find( 'series' ).each(function( i ) {
    var $this = $( this );
    chartConfigOptions.series[i] = {};
    chartConfigOptions.series[i].data = [];
    chartConfigOptions.series[i].name = $this.find( 'name' ).text();
    var points = $this.find( 'points' )[0].innerHTML.split( ',' );
    for ( var j in points ) {
      chartConfigOptions.series[i].data.push( parseInt( points[j] ) );
    }
  });
  if ( $( '#climate_data' ).highcharts() ) {
    $( '#climate_data' ).highcharts().destroy();
  }
  $( '#climate_data' ).highcharts( chartConfigOptions );
});
```

We first retrieve the XML file using the jQuery's `$.get()` method. The file contents are passed as an argument to the callback function that we wrap inside the jQuery object and assign to a variable named `xml`. We then iterate through each series element inside and create a new empty series object at index `i` of the `chartConfigOptions.series` array. At the same time, we also assign an empty `data` array to this object and give a value to the `name` property of the series.

In the next step, we find the `points` element and split its value using the comma (,) delimiter. This splitting results in an array that we call `points`. We then iterate over the values of `points` and push them into the `data` array of the current series.

Before loading the chart, we check and destroy any previously loaded chart into the container. Finally, we load the current chart with new data into the container.

Since the data is the same for the current and the previous example, the charts produced are also identical.

Preprocessing data from a JSON file

Parsing a **JavaScript Object Notation (JSON)** file in JavaScript is relatively easy since it's natively a JavaScript object. We can iterate through its properties just as we iterate through a normal JavaScript object.

In the following example, we will be using the same data as the previous two examples and plotting a line chart by preprocessing data from a JSON file.

The JSON file has data in the following format:

```
{
  "series": [
   {
      "name": "Maximum",
      "data": [80,70,76,79,...]
   },
   {
     ...
   },
   {
     ...
   }
  ]
}
```

The `series` array is wrapped inside a top-level object and it contains multiple objects with `name` and `data` properties. The `name` property is a string, while the `data` property is an array that contains data points.

The code to retrieve the JSON file and then plot the chart is as follows:

```
$.getJSON( 'climate-july-14.json', function( data ) {
   chartConfigOptions.series = data.series;

   if ( $( '#climate_data' ).highcharts() ) {
```

```
    $( '#climate_data' ).highcharts().destroy();
  }

    $( '#climate_data' ).highcharts( chartConfigOptions );
});
```

We first get the JSON file using the jQuery's `$.getJSON()` method that accepts the path of JSON file as the first argument. The parsed data is then passed to a callback function as an argument. Since the structure of `data.series` is the same as required for `series` in Highcharts' configuration object, we assigned `data.series` to `chartConfigOptions.series`.

In the next step, we destroyed any previously loaded chart in the container and initialized a new chart by passing the `chartConfigOptions` object.

Referring to the preceding steps in which we initialized a chart by loading the data from a JSON file, it becomes clear that the JSON format requires the most minimal steps for data preprocessing.

In this section, we learned to preprocess data contained in static files. In the next section, we will learn to retrieve and preprocess data from a database using a server-side programming language.

Preprocessing data from a database using PHP's PDO class

When working with large applications, data is usually saved in databases rather than static files. This data is retrieved by a server-side language to be served to the client. Further, Highcharts runs only on the client side and is completely independent of the technology that is used at the server side. Hence, any server-side language can be used to dynamically generate HTML and JavaScript to produce charts with Highcharts.

In this section, we will use a database to store data and a server-side language (PHP) to retrieve that data. Due to the vast variety of databases available today, we will use PHP's PDO class that is a consistent interface to access twelve different types of databases; MySQL is one of them. The advantage of using this interface is that we can use the same functions to issue queries and fetch data, regardless of the type of database we use. You can find more about PDO at `http://php.net/manual/en/intro.pdo.php`.

The database we are using in this example is a popular MySQL Sakila database, that is widely used in educational material. This database contains sample data for an online DVD store. The data includes movies, actors, customers, inventory, and their relationships.

In order to follow this example, you will need to have WAMP, LAMP, or XAMPP installed as we will use PHP with MySQL. If you don't have these stacks installed, you can download and install them by visiting their respective sites:

- `http://www.wampserver.com/en/`
- `https://www.apachefriends.org/index.html`
- `https://bitnami.com/stack/lamp/installer`

You will also need to download the Sakila database from the following link under the **Example Databases** section:

`http://dev.mysql.com/doc/index-other.html`

Once you have downloaded the archive file, you can install it by importing it in `phpmyadmin` or via the MySQL console. We are not going to cover those steps here since they are outside the scope of this book. If you need help installing the database, you can follow the steps given at `http://dev.mysql.com/doc/sakila/en/sakila-installation.html`.

Fetching data and plotting the chart

Create a new file `index.php` and paste the following HTML code in it:

```
<!doctype html>
<html lang="en">
  <head>
    <meta charset="UTF-8">
    <title>Highcharts Essentials</title>
  </head>
  <body>
    <div id="actor_movies" style="width: 850px; height:
      450px;"></div>
    <script src="http://ajax.googleapis.com/ajax/libs/jquery/
      1.10.1/jquery.min.js"></script>
    <script src="js/highcharts.js"></script>
    <script>
      (function() {

      })();
    </script>
  </body>
</html>
```

The basic configuration object for our chart is as follows:

```
var chartConfigOptions = {
  title: {
    text: 'Most Number of Movies by Actors'
  },
  chart: {
    type: 'column'
  },
  tooltip: {
    valueSuffix: ' Movies',
    useHTML: true
  },
  xAxis: {
    title: {
      text: 'Actor'
    }
  },
  yAxis: {
    title: {
      text: 'Movies'
    }
  },
  series: [{
    name: 'Actors'
  }]
};
```

We have not yet defined any `categories` on the `xAxis` component and `data` in the `series` as we are going to fetch it before inserting into the configuration object.

We will first fetch the data from the database using the PDO class and save it inside a variable. The PHP code is as follows:

```
<?php
  try {
    $con = new PDO( 'mysql:dbname=sakila;host=localhost', '$username',
'$password' );

    $data = $con->query( 'SELECT first_name, last_name, COUNT(film_
actor.actor_id)
      FROM film_actor
      JOIN actor
      ON film_actor.actor_id = actor.actor_id
      GROUP BY film_actor.actor_id
```

```
        ORDER BY COUNT(film_actor.actor_id) DESC
        LIMIT 10' );
    } catch ( PDOException $e ) {
      echo 'Connection failed: ' . $e->getMessage();
    }
  ?>
```

In order to better deal with errors and exceptions, we have wrapped our code to connect to the database inside a `try-catch` statement. Inside the `try` statement, we initialized the connection using the constructor method of the PDO class. The constructor method accepts a string as the first argument that contains the PDO driver name followed by a colon, the name of the database, and, finally, the host. The PDO driver name, the database name, and the host are `mysql`, `sakila`, and `localhost`, respectively. Your details may vary depending upon the environment you are working in. Next comes the `$username` and the `$password` as the second and third arguments; these are the username and password required to access the database.

The constructor method returns a PDO object upon connection success, which works as the connection handler. In our case, it is stored in the `$con` variable.

In the next step, we execute the query to retrieve the first name, last name, and the film count of the top ten actors. This list is sorted in descending order by the number of films done by each actor. We use the SQL `COUNT()` method to count the number of films using `actor_id` in the `film_actor` table. Since we also need to show the first and last names, we use the SQL `JOIN` clause to retrieve them from the `actor` table of the database. The results are limited to 10 and are stored in the `$data` variable for later use.

If the connection fails, PDO throws an exception that is caught by the `catch()` statement, in which case we show the error message using the `getMessage()` method of the `$e` exception object.

Next comes the JavaScript part of our code that handles the chart initialization. It is as follows:

```
var categories = [], data = [];

<?php
  foreach( $data as $row ) {
    $actor = $row;
    echo 'categories.push("' . $actor['first_name'] . '");';
```

```
        echo 'data.push(' . $actor['COUNT(film_actor.actor_id)'] . ');';
    }
?>

var chartConfigOptions = {
  title: {
    text: 'Most Number of Movies by Actors'
  },
  chart: {
    type: 'column'
  },
  tooltip: {
    valueSuffix: ' Movies',
    useHTML: true
  },
  xAxis: {
    title: {
      text: 'Actor'
    },
    categories: categories
  },
  yAxis: {
    title: {
      text: 'Movies'
    }
  },
  series: [{
    name: 'Actors',
    data: data
  }]
};

$( '#actor_movies' ).highcharts( chartConfigOptions );
```

We first initialize two empty arrays, that is `categories` and `data`, to hold *x* axis categories and series data. In the next step, we loop through `$data` to fetch the results row by row. In each iteration, we assign the current `$row` to the `$actor` variable. Although this is not necessary, we do so for better readability of our code. We then echo a PHP statement containing JavaScript's `push()` method to push an actor name `$actor['first_name']` to the `categories` array. This statement will be parsed as JavaScript once it renders on the page. Similarly, we push the movie count—`$actor['COUNT(film_actor.actor_id)']`—to the `data` array. This way, we have our `categories` and `data` arrays ready and can use them to define the categories and data for our chart.

In the next step, we initialize the configuration object for our chart. We use the same `categories` and `data` arrays to define `xAxis.categories` and `series.data`. Finally, we load the chart into its container.

The following chart is produced as a result of the preceding code:

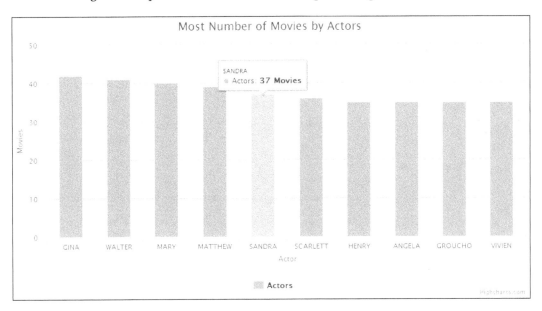

In this section, we used a server-side programming language to fetch the data from a database and render the chart. In the next section, we will learn to load data dynamically into the chart using Ajax.

Updating charts using Ajax

The retrieval of data from the server can be either by data-push or data-pull technologies. Since these topics are outside the scope of this book, we will limit ourselves to basic Ajax techniques. With Ajax, we can update a chart without the need to reload the whole page. This feature can be used to update charts when new data becomes available on the server.

In the following example, we will use Ajax to get data and update an already initialized chart at the click of a button. Contrary to the previous example, we will not mix our PHP and JavaScript code in this case, but rather will keep them in two separate files for better maintainability and readability.

We will use the same database and the same data as the previous example for the purpose of elaboration. Initially, our chart will be loaded with some random data. This can be considered as an initial state with the chart showing old data. As soon as an event occurs (in this case, a click), the client (browser) will request new data from the server; upon receiving that data, it will update the chart.

Initially, the chart is loaded with the current configuration:

```
var chartConfigOptions = {
  title: {
    text: 'Most Number of Movies by Actors'
  },
  chart: {
    type: 'column'
  },
  tooltip: {
    valueSuffix: ' Movies',
    useHTML: true
  },
  xAxis: {
    title: {
      text: 'Actor'
    },
    id: 'actor-names',
    categories: ['Jane', 'John', 'Doe']
  },
  yAxis: {
    title: {
      text: 'Movies'
    }
  },
  series: [{
    name: 'Actors',
    id: 'movie-count',
    data: [20, 10, 16]
  }]
};
$( '#actor_movies' ).highcharts( chartConfigOptions );
```

This will produce a simple column chart as shown in the following:

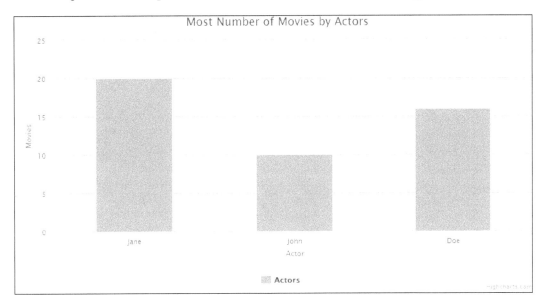

We begin working on the Ajax part by creating the `retrieve-data.php` file that will contain PHP code to handle data retrieval from the database.

We create a new button in our main HTML as follows:

```
<button data-action="retrieve_data">Retrieve New Data</button>
```

The code for `data-retrieval.php` is as follows:

```php
<?php

if( isset( $_POST ) ) {
  try {
    $con = new PDO( 'mysql:dbname=sakila;host=localhost', 'root', ''
);
    $results = $con->query( 'SELECT first_name, last_name, COUNT(film_
actor.actor_id)
    FROM film_actor
    JOIN actor
    ON film_actor.actor_id = actor.actor_id
    GROUP BY film_actor.actor_id
    ORDER BY COUNT(film_actor.actor_id) DESC
    LIMIT 10' );
  } catch ( PDOException $e ) {
    echo 'Connection failed: ' . $e->getMessage();
```

```
    }

    if( isset( $results ) ) {
      $data = [];
      $categories = [];
      $combined = [];

      foreach( $results as $row ) {
        array_push( $categories, $row['first_name'] );
        array_push( $data, (int) $row['COUNT(film_actor.actor_id)'] );
      }

      array_push( $combined, $data );
      array_push( $combined, $categories );

      header( 'Content-Type: application/json' );
      echo json_encode( $combined );
    }
  }
```

We start by checking the $_POST super global variable to determine whether a request has been made. Next, inside a try-catch statement, we establish the connection to the database and execute a query just as we did in the previous example. If the query is successful, the results will be returned to the $results variable.

In the next step, we check whether any results have been returned by checking the $results variable. If there are returned results, we initialize two variables, that is $data and $categories, to hold series data and axis categories.

By iterating over $results, we collect categories and data in their separate arrays using PHP's array_push() method. Note that, in the case of $data, we typecast the current data point to an integer using (int). This is due to the fact that data can be interpreted as a string when fetching results from a query. Since we echoed the data inline in the previous example within the JavaScript code, typecasting it to an integer was not required there.

When both $data and $categories arrays are ready, we combine them into a single array, $combined, which we initialized earlier. In the next step, we set the header to JSON and echo out JSON representation of the $combined array. We will now write the JavaScript code to handle the request and receive JSON data from the server.

Since the request will initiate on the button click, we wrap our code inside an event handler method of click event for the button:

```
$( '[data-action="retrieve_data"]' ).on( 'click', function( e ) {
  e.preventDefault();
  $.ajax({
    type: 'POST',
    url: 'retrieve-data.php',
    beforeSend: function() {
      $( '#actor_movies' ).highcharts().showLoading();
    },
    success: function( data ) {
      var axis = $( '#actor_movies' ).highcharts().get( 'actor-names' ),
        series = $( '#actor_movies' ).highcharts().get( 'movie-count' );

      axis.setCategories( data[1], false );
      series.setData( data[0], false );
      $( '#actor_movies' ).highcharts().redraw();
    },
    complete: function() {
      $( '#actor_movies' ).highcharts().hideLoading();
    }
  })
});
```

In the preceding code, we send an Ajax request to the server using the `jQuery.ajax()` method. It accepts an object containing various properties of the request including the `type` and the `url` properties.

The `beforeSend()` function fires before sending the request and chart loading is shown using Highcharts' `Chart.showLoading()` method.

Upon success of the request, the `success()` method fires and accepts the returned data as the argument. The `data` returned from the server is composed of two arrays containing data points and categories, respectively.

Next, using the `Chart.get()` method, we get the axis and series by using their IDs. Their references are stored in the `axis` and `series` variables, respectively.

In the next step, we set the axis categories and series data using the `Axis.setCategories()` and `Series.setData()` methods. In both of the methods, we set the second `redraw` argument to `false` as we manually redraw the chart using the `Chart.redraw()` method.

Finally, the `complete()` callback fires after the invocation of the `success` (or `error`) method. At this point, we remove the chart loading using the `Chart.hideLoading()` method.

You can learn more about the `jQuery.ajax()` method by visiting the following link:

`http://api.jquery.com/jQuery.ajax/`

The chart produced after clicking on the button is the same as the previous example.

In this section, we learned to create Ajax requests to receive data from the server and dynamically update the chart with new data. We used a couple of Highcharts API methods including `Axis.setCategories()` and `Series.setData()`. In the next section, we will learn about Highcharts' export module.

Exporting Highcharts into other formats

Highcharts provides a module to export charts into various image formats. There can be two possibilities when considering the export server, that is, to use Highcharts' official exporting server or set up your own server. We will use the export module to export our charts into various formats using the Highcharts CDN.

To enable exporting, the `exporting.js` file must be included after the `highcharts.js` file. It can be found in the `Highcharts-4.x.x/js/modules` folder and can also be included directly from `http://code.highcharts.com/modules/exporting.js`.

To enable simple exporting, we need to set `exporting.enabled` to `true` in our chart configuration object:

```
$( '...' ).highcharts({
  ...
  exporting: {
    enabled: true
  },
  ...
});
```

By doing so, a button with a drop-down menu appears at the top-right corner of the chart:

The drop-down menu contains various options to export charts into formats including PNG, JPEG, PDF, and SVG.

You can alter various properties including image width and height, filename, and the URL of the exporting server. Button properties can also be changed within the chart by referring to `exporting.buttons.contextButton`.

You can find more about the exporting module at `http://api.highcharts.com/highcharts#exporting`.

Exporting charts programmatically

In addition to exporting the context button, we can also export charts programmatically using Highcharts or a local export server.

In the following example, we will export a chart by passing the basic configuration object in an Ajax request to the server. The data sent to the server in the Ajax request contains parameters for the configuration object and file attributes.

The following code elaborates a simple request sent to Highcharts' exporting server:

```
var chartConfigJSON = {
  "chart": {
    "type": "line"
  },
  "xAxis": {
    "categories": ['Jane', 'John', 'Doe']
  },
  "series": [{
```

```
      "name": "Persons",
      "data": [20, 45, 30]
   }]
};

var requestString = "async=true&type=pdf&width=500&options=" + JSON.
stringify( chartConfigJSON );

$.ajax({
   type: 'POST',
   data: requestString,
   url: 'http://export.highcharts.com',
   success: function( filename ) {
      window.open( 'http://export.highcharts.com/' + filename );
   }
});
```

We first define a JSON object with the same structure as the Highcharts configuration object and call it `chartConfigJSON`. In the next step, we define another variable `requestString` that contains post parameters appended by the JSON string of `chartConfigJSON`. We used a JavaScript method `JSON.stringify()` that converts a JSON to a string.

Next, we post an Ajax request to `http://export.highcharts.com` containing previously defined parameters. The success function receives the path of the file at Highcharts' export server, which we open in a new window for the user.

Summary

In the concluding chapter, we learned various techniques to work with Highcharts data and data preprocessing. We looked at loading data from various file formats and formatting it to be plotted with Highcharts. We also learned to interact with a database using a server-side programming language to retrieve data and dynamically plot charts with Ajax. In the final section of this chapter, we learned about Highcharts' export module that can be used to export Highcharts into various file formats.

I hope that this book proved useful in your journey of learning Highcharts. We have covered numerous topics in this book, essential ones as well as the new features, which come packed with the new version of Highcharts, such as 3D charts, heat maps, and gauges. From basic chart types to their derivatives along with their combinations, everything has been explained in plain language to help you grasp the concepts easily. As for intermediate techniques, we have explored Highcharts APIs and events to further enhance user interactions. To further explore the topics that were not covered in this book, you can always refer to the official documentation at `http://api.highcharts.com/highcharts`.

With this, I thank you for reading this book and for your support. I hope to bring yet another book to explore more advanced Highcharts concepts. Till then, Good bye!

Index

Symbol

3D pie chart
  creating 89

A

addEvent() method 182
addSeries event 181
Ajax
  used, for updating chart 197-201
alpha property 36
angular gauge chart
  creating 111, 112
  styling 114-116
  with dual axes 113, 114
APIs, Highcharts
  overview 160-163
area charts
  about 61
  creating, with missing values of series 65
  creating, with multiple series 63, 64
  creating, with percentage values 72
  example 61, 62
  modifying 69-71
  stacking, with multiple series 67-69
  tick mark placement, adjusting 63
  tooltip, sharing between multiple series 66
area-spline charts 73
axis, chart
  extreme values, setting 175
Axis class
  addPlotBand() method 160
  getExtremes() method 160
  setCategories() method 160
  URL 160
Axis.setExtremes() method
  used, for setting extreme values on axis 175

B

backgrounds
  altering 140, 141
bar charts 30-34
borders
  altering 140, 141
bubble charts
  creating 78-80

C

Character Separated Values. *See* **Comma Separated Values (CSV)**
chart
  configuring, for internationalization 156, 157
  destroying 179
  drilling down 25-28
  global theme, creating for 151-155
  reflowing 177, 178
  updating, Ajax used 197-201
chart.addPoint() method
  about 169
  URL, for documentation 169
chart.addSeries() method
  about 172
  URL 171
  using 169
chart animation
  disabling 163

Chart class
  about 160
  addAxis() method 160
  addSeries() method 160
  destroy() method 160
  getSVG() method 160
  URL 160
chart.drillUp() method 175
chart elements
  adjusting 29
Chart.get() method
  using 164, 165
chart.reflow() method
  used, for reflowing chart 177, 178
class model, Highcharts
  about 159
  Axis 160
  Chart 160
  chart animation, disabling 163
  overview 160-163
  Point 160
  Renderer 160
  Series 160
click event 181
colorAxis.marker property 129
colorByPoint property 135
color property 39, 71
column charts
  about 15-18
  and line charts, combining 57-59
  Highcharts official documentation,
      using 18
  normal stacking 20
  percentage stacking 20
  pie charts, combining with 97-100
  stacking 20
  with normal stacking 20-22
  with percentage stacking 22, 23
columns
  gradient background, used for 143
Comma Separated Values (CSV)
  about 186
  data, preprocessing 186-188
custom event handlers
  adding 182

D

data
  loading, from HTML table 52-54
data labels
  formatting 44-46
data, preprocessing
  from CSV file 186-188
  from database, PDO class
      used 192, 193
  from different file types 185
  from JSON file 191, 192
  from XML file 189, 190
date/time
  formatting 44-46
dateTimeLabelFormats object 45
Date.UTC() method 43, 49
directory, Highcharts
  examples 11
  exporting-server 11
  gfx 11
  graphics 11
  index.html 10
  js 11
div tag 139
donut chart
  creating 92-94
drilldown event 181
drilldown property 87
drillup event 181
duration property 150

E

easing property 150
Element class 161
events, Highcharts
  about 181
  addSeries event 181
  click event 181
  drilldown event 181
  drillup event 181
  load event 181
  redraw event 181
  reference link 181
  selection event 181

exporting module, Highcharts
URL 203
eXtensible Markup Language (XML) 189

F

fillColor property 71
fillOpacity property 71
fine-tuning, appearance 130, 131
formatter() method
  about 47, 131, 139
  URL 34
funnel chart
  drawing 125-127

G

global theme
  creating, for charts 151-155
Google Fonts
  used, with Highcharts 148-150
Google Translate
  URL 156
Google Web Fonts
  URL 148
gradient fill types
  about 141
  gradient background, for columns 143, 144
  gradient background, for tooltips 143, 144
  linear gradients 141, 142
  linear gradients, with multiple color
      stops 145
  radial gradients 146
  radial gradients, applying to pie
      chart 147, 148

H

heat map
  creating 127-129
  fine-tuning, appearance 130, 131
  tooltip, formatting 131, 132
Highcharts
  about 7
  custom event handlers, adding 182
  example 12-14
  exporting, into other formats 202

exporting, programmatically 203, 204
extending 181
Google Fonts, used with 148-150
installing 9-11
prototype functions, wrapping 183
selecting 7
URL 9
URL, for extending 183
Highcharts.dateFormat() method 47
Highcharts documentation
  URL 9, 18
Highcharts drilldown feature
  URL 29
Highcharts, features
  browser support 8
  chart types, defining 7
  data, preprocessing 8
  dynamic 8
  extensibility 9
  multilingual 8
  responsive 8
  theming support 8
Highcharts.wrap() method 183
HTML
  tooltip, formatting with 137-140
HTML table
  data, loading from 52-54

I

innerSize property 94
internationalization
  charts, configuring for 156, 157
irregular time intervals
  line charts, creating with 48-50

J

JavaScript Object Notation (JSON) 191
jQuery.ajax() method
  URL 202
jQuery UI easing
  used, for series animation 150, 151
js directory
  adapters 11
  modules 11
  themes 11

JSON file
  data, preprocessing 191, 192

L

LAMP
  URL, for downloading 193
lang component
  about 88
  URL, for documentation 88
legend component 153
linearGradient object 142
linear gradients
  about 141, 142
  applying, to pie chart 147, 148
  with multiple color stops 145
line charts
  about 41
  and column charts, combining 57-59
  creating, with irregular time intervals 48-50
  creating, with multiple series 50-52
  creating, with regular time intervals 42-44
  pie charts, combining with 97-100
line charts, regular time intervals
  data labels, formatting 44-46
  date/time, formatting 44-46
  tooltip, formatting 47, 48
lineColor property 71
load event 181

M

multiple color stops
  linear gradients, used with 145
multiple data series
  including 18-20
multiple series
  line charts, creating with 50-52

N

neckHeight property 126
neckWidth property 126
negatively stacked bar charts 34
normal stacking 20-22

O

opposite:true property 156

P

pane component
  URL 112
Papa Parse
  about 186
  URL, for documentation 186
PDO
  URL 192
PDO class
  data, fetching 193-197
  data, plotting on chart 193-197
  used, for preprocessing data from
      database 192, 193
percentage stacking 22, 23
pie charts
  3D pie chart, creating 89
  about 81
  back button, modifying 88
  combining, with column charts 97-100
  combining, with line charts 97-100
  creating 82-84
  creating, with multiple series 90, 91
  drilling 86, 87
  radial gradient, applying to 147, 148
  slicing, by point selection 85, 86
  slicing off 84
plot bands
  spline charts, creating with 56, 57
**plotOptions.column.groupZPadding
      property 36**
plotOptions component
  URL 21
Point class
  about 160
  series property 160
  URL, for documentation 160
pointFormat property
  about 76, 84
  used, for formatting scatter chart tooltip 76
points
  adding, dynamically 166-169

polar chart
  about 100
  creating 101, 102
  creating, with different series types 103
  other chart types, converting to 104, 105
preprocessing 185
Producer Price Index (PPI) 54
prototype functions
  wrapping 183
pyramid chart
  plotting 124, 125

R

radial gradients 146
redraw event 181
regular time intervals
  line charts, creating with 42-44
Renderer class
  about 160
  URL 160

S

Sakila database
  URL, for downloading 193
Scalable Vector Graphics (SVG) 8
scatter charts
  about 74, 75
  creating, with multiple series 76
  tooltip, formatting with pointFormat
    property 75
selection event 181
semicircle donut chart
  creating 95-97
series
  adding, dynamically 169, 170
  displaying 180
  drilldowns, adding to 171-174
  drilling up 175
  excluding, from stacking 24
  hiding 180
series animation
  jQuery UI easing, used for 150, 151
Series class
  about 160

addPoint() method 160
  chart property 160
  hide() method 160
  show() method 160
  URL 160
series.hide() method
  used, for hiding series 180
series.show() method
  used, for displaying series 180
shadows
  altering 140, 141
size property 39, 94
slice property 84
solid gauge
  creating 119-121
speedometers 111
spider web chart
  about 105
  creating 105
spline charts
  creating 54
  creating, with plot bands 56, 57
stacking
  series, excluding from 24
stacking, area charts
  with multiple series 67-69
standalone easing plugin
  URL 150
style attribute 139
subtitle property 17

T

theming 134-136
this.series.color property 139
this.series.name property 52, 139
tickInterval property 29
  URL 45
tickmarkPlacement property
  about 63
  URL, for documentation 63
ticks
  adjusting 29
title, chart
  setting 176
title property 17

tooltip
  formatting 46-48, 131, 132
  formatting, with HTML 137-140
  gradient background, used for 143
type property 43

V

Vector Markup Language (VML) 8
viewing frame
  modifying 38, 39
VU meter
  creating 117-119

W

WAMP
  URL, for downloading 193
waterfall chart
  plotting 121-123
width property 130
wind rose chart
  creating 107-109

X

XAMPP
  URL, for downloading 193
XML file
  data, preprocessing 189, 190

Y

yAxis component 113

Thank you for buying
Highcharts Essentials

About Packt Publishing

Packt, pronounced 'packed', published its first book *"Mastering phpMyAdmin for Effective MySQL Management"* in April 2004 and subsequently continued to specialize in publishing highly focused books on specific technologies and solutions.

Our books and publications share the experiences of your fellow IT professionals in adapting and customizing today's systems, applications, and frameworks. Our solution based books give you the knowledge and power to customize the software and technologies you're using to get the job done. Packt books are more specific and less general than the IT books you have seen in the past. Our unique business model allows us to bring you more focused information, giving you more of what you need to know, and less of what you don't.

Packt is a modern, yet unique publishing company, which focuses on producing quality, cutting-edge books for communities of developers, administrators, and newbies alike. For more information, please visit our website: www.packtpub.com.

About Packt Open Source

In 2010, Packt launched two new brands, Packt Open Source and Packt Enterprise, in order to continue its focus on specialization. This book is part of the Packt Open Source brand, home to books published on software built around Open Source licenses, and offering information to anybody from advanced developers to budding web designers. The Open Source brand also runs Packt's Open Source Royalty Scheme, by which Packt gives a royalty to each Open Source project about whose software a book is sold.

Writing for Packt

We welcome all inquiries from people who are interested in authoring. Book proposals should be sent to author@packtpub.com. If your book idea is still at an early stage and you would like to discuss it first before writing a formal book proposal, contact us; one of our commissioning editors will get in touch with you.

We're not just looking for published authors; if you have strong technical skills but no writing experience, our experienced editors can help you develop a writing career, or simply get some additional reward for your expertise.

Learning Highcharts

ISBN: 978-1-84951-908-3   Paperback: 362 pages

Create rich, intuitive, and interactive JavaScript data visualization for your web and enterprise development needs using this powerful charting library — Highcharts

1. Step-by-step instructions with real-live data to create bar charts, column charts, and pie charts to easily create artistic and professional quality charts.

2. Learn tips and tricks to create a variety of charts such as horizontal gauge charts, projection charts, and circular ratio charts.

3. Use and integrate Highcharts with jQuery Mobile and ExtJS 4, and understand how to run Highcharts on the server-side.

Highcharts Cookbook

ISBN: 978-1-78355-968-8   Paperback: 332 pages

80 hands-on recipes to create, integrate, and extend dynamic and interactive charts in your web projects

1. Create amazing interactive charts that update in real time.

2. Make charts that work wherever you go: phone or desktop, online or offline.

3. Learn how to extend and enhance Highcharts to design and develop charts easily.

Please check **www.PacktPub.com** for information on our titles

Instant Highcharts

ISBN: 978-1-84969-754-5   Paperback: 50 pages

Learn to create dynamic and customized charts
instantly using Highcharts

1. Learn something new in an Instant!
    A short, fast, focused guide delivering
    immediate results.

2. Create your first customized and
    interactive Highcharts.

3. Get to grips with the core concepts
    of Highcharts.

Learning jqPlot

ISBN: 978-1-78398-116-8   Paperback: 240 pages

Learn how to create your very own rich and intuitive
JavaScript data visualizations using jqPlot

1. Learn the fundamentals and applications
    of jqPlot as you work as a data analyst for
    a fictional consumer electronics company.

2. Build on and extend the examples that you
    follow throughout the book and build your
    own complex and interesting charts.

3. Accessible for anyone because knowledge of
    similar tools such as Highcharts isn't required.

Please check **www.PacktPub.com** for information on our titles

www.ingramcontent.com/pod-product-compliance
Lightning Source LLC
LaVergne TN
LVHW081340050326
832903LV00024B/1232